CAREERS
F O R
NATURE
LOVERS
& Other
Outdoor Types

CAREERS

FOR

NATURE LOVERS

& Other Outdoor Types

Louise Miller

VGM Career Horizons
a division of *NTC Publishing Group*
Lincolnwood, Illinois USA

Dedication

To the privilege of sharing life with two members of another (thankfully not endangered) species—Baby and Buster, my daily connection with nature at its loving best.

Library of Congress Cataloging-in-Publication Data
Miller, Louise, 1940–
    Careers for nature lovers & other outdoor types / Louise Miller.
        p.   cm. — (VGM careers for you series)
    ISBN 0-8442-8132-8 :   — ISBN 0-8442-8133-6 (pbk.)   :
    1. Conservation of natural resources—Vocational guidance.
2. Environmental protection—Vocational guidance.   3. Biology— Vocational guidance.   I. Title.   II. Title: Careers for nature lovers and other outdoor types.
III. Series.
S945.M55   1992
333.7'2'023—dc20   91-46081
                                                                            CIP

1993 Printing

Published by VGM Career Horizons, a division of NTC Publishing Group.
© 1992 by NTC Publishing Group, 4255 West Touhy Avenue,
Lincolnwood (Chicago), Illinois 60646-1975 U.S.A.

 3 4 5 6 7 8 9 0 VP 9 8 7 6 5 4 3 2

Contents

About the Author

Along with the rest of you, the author is concerned with the preservation of the planet and the conservation of natural resources. Besides recycling, shopping carefully, and not eating meat, Miller is also trying to spread the word about restoration, reusing, and repair.

In addition to nature, Miller also loves languages, especially English and German. She started out as a German teacher and teaches it today, after having studied in Vienna, Austria, and Bonn, Germany. She has also taught German at the Universities of Kansas, Missouri, and Illinois.

Her love of English led her to teaching, writing, editing, and proofreading the language. She has taught English at community and business colleges, has conducted writing workshops, and has worked both full time and free-lance for publishing houses. These include New Horizons Publishers, Compton's Encyclopedia, Rand McNally & Company, Richard D. Irwin, American Library Association, National Institute of Real Estate Brokers, and World Book. Miller was also research coordinator for television quiz shows in Los Angeles and has written a regular wildlife column for the Woodstock (Illinois) *Sentinel.*

Foreword

With environmental issues such as global warming, ozone depletion, and tropical deforestation increasingly in the news, it should come as no surprise that Americans are more concerned about the environment than ever before. For the first time, Americans are realizing that our quality of life depends largely on the quality of the environment. And more and more people want to do something about it.

This interest in environmental issues may be recent, but our appreciation for nature is nothing new. We have always valued the scenic beauty of our national parks, forests, and natural areas. We treasure the diversity of plants and animals that inhabit these unspoiled places. And we find a special tranquility and connection with nature in these settings.

If you share this love of nature—and share the desire to preserve the natural world—you may wish to transform your interest into a career. *Careers for Nature Lovers* can help by offering information on a wide array of jobs in fields as diverse as biology, agriculture, land management, forestry, geology, and waste management. What's more, these aren't office jobs—as you will discover, this book focuses on employment opportunities that actually involve working outdoors.

You'll find details about jobs for geoscientists who study natural disasters such as earthquakes and for pollution control technicians who monitor industry's compliance with government pollution regulations. You'll find out about jobs for zoologists who work to save endangered species and for foresters who manage our national parks. Not only do these professions get you outside, working on the ground, but they can also make a crucial difference in stemming the environmental degradation that threatens our magnificent natural heritage.

I often tell people that being president of The Nature Conservancy is the best job in the world, in large part because I get to travel frequently to the Conservancy's system of 1,300 nature preserves in the United States and its cooperative projects beyond our borders. But when I'm visiting these beautiful places, I usually find myself envious of the preserve managers and land stewards. These are the people who are really on the cutting edge of environmental protection. Men and women working *in* the outdoors *for* the outdoors are the ones who are getting things done and making a difference for us and for generations to come.

John C. Sawhill
President
The Nature Conservancy

CHAPTER ONE

The Wonderful World of Nature

Y ou are probably among the many Americans who are now recycling newspapers, plastic products, tin cans, and glass bottles. Maybe you have even started to cut back on your use of water, use cloth instead of paper napkins or disposable diapers, and buy only biodegradable detergents and cleaning materials. You carpool, walk, bike, or use public transportation; bring your own cloth bags to the grocery store; and use potpourri to sweeten your home instead of spray deodorizers. You order from Seventh Generation catalog, have switched to wearing cotton instead of synthetics. You may even use rechargeable batteries and compact fluorescent instead of incandescent light bulbs. Your stationery, wrapping paper, and greeting cards are made from recycled paper, and you buy only organically grown fruits and vegetables.

Your memberships include Greenpeace, the Sierra Club, the Wildlife Society, The Nature Conservancy, and the National Wildlife Federation. You are concerned about endangered species, the greenhouse effect, the rain forests, the global deterioration of ecosystems, and the wild animals who are being displaced from their natural habitats because of land development. You may even have become a vegetarian or quit smoking to conserve resources and to clean up your own and others' breathing space.

You have devoured books and magazine articles with hints on how to change your daily habits to renew the earth and avoid cruelty to animals. In addition, you have picketed, written to your senator or representative in Congress, have attended public hearings, and tried to convert your neighbors and friends to recycle and become aware of the world around them before it is too late.

You are probably doing all these things because you are worried about the environment, that is, all the components of the natural world that must be shared, preserved, conserved, and protected. Concern for the earth, the air we breathe, animals, fish, plants, the food we eat, the water we drink—the resources of this planet that are necessary for life to be sustained—has become part of your thought process and life-style on a daily basis.

Most of us are becoming more aware that some of the natural resources that have been available all our lives may not be here for our children or grandchildren. We are also becoming increasingly aware that we hold in our hands the power to change—even to reverse—the damage that has been done to the environment if we all act in concert in everyday ways for the rest of our lives.

Working to Save the Earth

You may even be one of those who chooses to make a career of your love of and concern for nature. You may be a person who wants to pursue even further the extent to which you can contribute to the preservation of the natural resources that once were so abundant but now may be threatened. If you are at the point in your life where you would literally like to "save the earth," you may be interested in exploring the many jobs available to you. Many nature lovers work in laboratories and offices, schools and universities. But we are going to concentrate on those careers whose primary focus has to do with the outdoors, literally working with Mother Nature.

Some of the jobs we will discuss require a high degree of education and training; others do not. Some emphasize work with the land; others may deal primarily with water, air, plants, or animals. Within the various categories, there may be a choice of location of workplace, such as the ocean, the mountains, or in a park. Some workplaces are in cities; others, on farms or ranches. Many jobs require a high degree of scientific knowledge and expertise. In those cases, your education will play a major factor in your decision.

The federal government offers a wide range of career opportunities in the environmental field. State, county, and municipal governmental agencies also offer jobs as well as independent agencies and organizations. More and more, corporations and industry throughout the world have departments that are singularly devoted to studying and analyzing the organization's compliance with environmental regulations.

We will see, as we explore the possibilities, a global concern for ecological and environmental matters, because what happens in the United States may affect Canada and Mexico, including air and water pollution. If a nuclear accident occurs in Russia, it may have effects on the rest of Europe and Asia. What happens in the rain forests of South America affects all life on earth, and a species that is endangered in Africa may affect the ecological balance of related life forms.

A worldwide approach is essential to the preservation and improvement of our natural environment also because of our advanced technology, increasing population, depletion of resources, destructive oil spills, and increasing possibilities of nuclear disaster. Nature can no longer cleanse itself, so we all have to do our part in order to restore the natural balance and order.

Is Environmental Work for You?

So you have started in your home, your neighborhood, at your school, or in your office to repair, recycle, reuse, and restore the man-made and natural resources under your personal control. But somewhere inside you may feel that that is not enough. Your interests lie in the larger picture. But where do you begin? You might start by asking yourself some basic questions:

1. Do I like to work outdoors under any weather condition, such as cold, snow, sleet, rain, or tropical heat?

2. Do I prefer to work with the study, analysis, and improvement of air, water, land, plants, or animals?

3. Which science courses have I had in school—earth science, biology, chemistry, zoology, botany?

4. Which science courses did I like the best?

5. Do I work well as a member of a team?

6. Am I physically strong and healthy?

7. Do I communicate well both orally and in writing?

8. Am I willing to relocate?

9. How much time am I willing to devote to further education and training?

10. Would I prefer to work for the government, a private conservation organization, or a corporation?

If changing or harsh weather conditions don't bother you, and you have decided in which area you want to work, you can proceed to questions 3 and 4. If you are still in high school and decide that you want to become a botanist, you should begin to investigate colleges and universities that will best suit your needs. Make sure that botany was your favorite science course first.

If you've ever played softball, volleyball, or football, you know whether you are a good team player. If you are still in school, you may also be a member of a debating team, glee club, or editorial staff. These are all teams of people who have to work harmoniously for a common goal. If you work in an office or have done volunteer work for a community organization or hospital, you also have been a team member. If you share information easily with others, if you give credit where it is due, and rejoice over a job well done (even if it has been done by someone else), you're a good team player. Different teams of scientists and experts often have to work together to solve an environmental problem on an interdisciplinary basis, so if you work well with others and are willing to share your results, you'll do fine.

Since outdoor jobs often require physical work under less than desirable or comfortable conditions, you may have to be more physically fit than you would for a more sedentary job. Now is the time to look at your health habits in order to be ready for the more strenuous future work outdoors.

As a member of an outdoor field team, you will have to know the terminology and even jargon of the particular science you're involved in to be able to communicate with others. You may also be called upon to write up the results and recommendations of your field investigations to present to your supervisor or to the public. Some computer literacy may be required for many of these jobs.

Some of the jobs you prefer may be located primarily in the West, and there you are in your office in New Jersey! More opportunities for, say, park rangers or agronomists may exist in the midwestern or western states, while aquatic biologists may find opportunities on either coast. So you may not want to invest in property anywhere until you really look into the chances for environmental work in your field.

If you are in either high school or college now, it is an excellent time to dig deep into your interests and aptitudes and adjust your curriculum accordingly, talk to career counselors, send off for university catalogs, write to local governmental agencies, check for grass-roots organizations in your hometown, read books and articles, and do volunteer work during the summer vacation in the field you think you're interested in. The more education and training you have, the better the chances for employment.

If you already have a career in another field but feel that you would like to change to an environmental career, you will also have to do a little soul-searching and investigating. First, determine which field you want to be in, the extent of education that is required for it, and specific education and training you will need to change careers. It may take another few years at night school to acquire the certificate, license, or degree that you need, but the time and effort will be well worth it because you will be doing what you really want to do for the rest of your life—and helping to save the earth as well.

Part of your investigation into careers will lead you to the three major employers: the government, private agencies, and industry. Each employer has its advantages and disadvantages, requirements, criteria, educational standards, and degrees of commitment—all of which should help you decide.

Types of Environmental Careers

So, with all this in mind, let's take a look at some of the opportunities available to you in this most important of career tracks—the preservation of Mother Earth and all her creatures!

Careers in Biology

If we define biology as the study of living things, we can see how all-encompassing careers in the biological sciences can be. They include everything from aquatic biologists to soil scientists, from botanists to toxicologists, from game managers to horticulturists. Biologists are employed in forests, agricultural research stations, ocean ships, and farms. If you choose biology for a career, you will need at least a high school diploma or bachelor's degree. With a master's degree or Ph.D., a solid, long-term career is almost assured. So start studying now to be a botanist, physiologist, biochemist, zoologist, ecologist, or horticulturist, and you are entering the wonderful world of the biological scientist. Your chances for a rewarding career are excellent.

Landscape Architecture

Landscape architects are on-site specialists in the analysis of land features, vegetation, and geography for use in the design of projects in forests, parks, and subdivisions and for airports and highways. Landscape architects are employed by local governments, corporations, or engineering firms. Others are self-employed, often as consultants.

Land developers work closely with landscape architects to assure that the land is suitable for the particular project that they are planning and that environmental regulations are complied with. In addition to a bachelor's degree, you may also need a state license if you want to practice independently.

Forestry Work

You may also want to consider the possibility of becoming a forest ranger or manager. Much of the United States is forest land, and a chief obligation of a forester is to prevent fires and to be generally responsible for the proper maintenance of the trees in a forest and the safety of visitors. The forest manager assumes larger responsibilities according to the uses of the forest, that is, whether the forest is used as a wildlife refuge or for the production of lumber.

Conservation scientists, such as fish culturists, wildlife biologists, technicians, wardens, and animal rehabilitators as well as ornithologists, ecologists, and wildlife managers, are also employed in parks and forests throughout the country. Since the forest houses so many different life forms and can be used for different purposes, you may find your niche here.

Geological Sciences

Geology and related geosciences may intrigue you as a possible career track. The government, private industry, architectural firms, oil companies—all employ geologists. More and more, geologists are becoming involved in environmental work, including pollution and waste management. A solid background in mathematics and science is necessary whether you decide to work as an engineering geologist, marine geologist, hydrologist, or mineralogist. A college degree is necessary, and a master's degree is required for some positions.

Waste Management and Pollution Control

Areas of environmental work that are becoming increasingly important are waste management and pollution control. Many efforts have been made over the past several years to try to alleviate the problems of open dumping of garbage into landfills. These dumps can eventually contaminate groundwater and provide a base for spreading disease.

There will always be garbage, but local governments and private organizations are employing engineers, chemists, toxicologists, inspectors, and analysts to become up with safe ideas for waste management and to try to recover energy and natural resources. Both government and private industry must also comply with a body of regulations that have been enacted to protect the environment. One way of dealing with waste is, of course, through recycling of plastic, glass, paper, and aluminum. A whole new avenue of careers has grown out of this aspect of waste management, and it also offers new career opportunities.

As we know, employment for the various careers working with the environment is available through federal, state, and local governments; private industry; and independent, grass-roots organizations. Federal employing agencies involved in some aspect of the environment are the Environmental Protection Agency, U.S. Fish and Wildlife Service, U.S. Forest Service, U.S. Bureau of Mines, Bureau of Land Reclamation, National Park

Service, U.S. Geological Survey, the Nuclear Regulatory Commission, and the Smithsonian Environmental Research Center. Individual states employ environmental workers in their departments of natural resources, environmental protection, fish and wildlife, ecology, or pollution control. County and municipal agencies often have similar offices.

Independent and grass-roots organizations, such as Greenpeace, Center for Neighborhood Technology, The Wilderness Society, Save-the-Redwoods League, Friends of the Earth, and the National Association of Environmental Professionals may also serve as valuable career sources in your pursuit of an environmental career. Private corporations advertise in local and national newspapers, trade publications, and professional newsletters.

Your local library should have a copy of *Encyclopedia of Associations,* which lists professional organizations within the various disciplines. They, in turn, may lead you to specific educational and training requirements as well as employment opportunities in your chosen field. The *Occupational Outlook Handbook* describes professions and projects future needs. College and university job placement services and counselors may put you in touch with recruiters from industries and agencies that are hiring.

So the keys for opening up doors to a new and important career are at your disposal. Let's walk into this vast hall of possibilities to see if we've come to the right place and what we're going to do when we get there.

For Further Information

Occupational Outlook Handbook. Bureau of Labor Statistics, Superintendent of Documents, U.S. Government Printing Office, Washington, DC
Careers. National Park Service, Department of the Interior, Washington, DC 20240
"Life Sciences Opportunities in the Federal Government," Announcement 421, rev. Aug. 1978, U.S. Office of Personnel Management, Washington, DC 20415

Careers in Environmental Protection. Reed Millard and the editors of Science Book Associates, Julia Messner, 1 West 39th Street, New York, NY 10018

Careers in Wildlife Conservation. John Madson and Ed Kosicky, Conservation Department, Olin Mathieson Chemical Corp., East Olin, IL 62024

Making a Living in Conservation—A Guide to Outdoor Careers. Albert M. Dacy, Stackpole Books, Cameron and Kelker Streets, Harrisburg, PA 17105

Environmental Job Opportunities. University of Wisconsin, 550 North Park Street, 15 Science Hall, Madison, WI 53706

Conservation Directory. National Wildlife Federation, 1412 Sixteenth Street, NW, Washington, DC 20036-2266

Complete Guide to Environmental Careers. The CEIP Fund, Inc., 68 Harrison Avenue, 5th Floor, Boston, MA 02111

Environmental Protection Careers Guidebook. U.S. Department of Labor, Employment and Training Administration and U.S. Environmental Protection Agency, EPA Office of Human Resources, Washington, DC

Michael Levine. *The Environmental Address Book.* New York: Perigee Books, 1991

Becoming an Environmental Professional 1990. The CEIP Fund, Inc., 68 Harrison Avenue, 5th Floor, Boston, MA 02116-1907

Canada-United States Environmental Council

Canada: Canadian Nature Federation
    75 Albert Street
    Ottawa, Ontario K2P 6G1

United States: c/o Defenders of Wildlife
    1244 19th Street, NW
    Washington, DC 20036

CHAPTER TWO

Careers in the Biological Sciences

T he field of biology is so wide-ranging that, if you choose a career in the biological sciences, you are assured of a variety of possibilities. These are not just confined to working with microscopes and formaldehyde, as you might think from your experience in high school classes.

If, for example, you choose to become a botanist, you'll be studying plant life; a zoologist, animal life; an ecologist, environmental relationships. As a physiologist, you would study life processes of living organisms.

If you want to work outdoors as a biologist, you may become a wildlife biologist or marine biologist, ornithologist or ichthyologist, herpetologist or mammalogist. You would work in forests and parks, zoos, agricultural research stations, at fish hatcheries, on ocean ships, or under water. You could also work at rehabilitation facilities.

Wildlife Biology Careers
Where Wildlife Biologists Work

As a wildlife biologist, you would probably work for the government—federal, state, or local. On the federal level, primary employers are the U.S. Fish and Wildlife Service of the Department of the Interior and the National Park Service. The U.S. Forest Service is also a possibility as well as the Bureau of Sport Fisheries and the National Marine Fishery Service. Every state has a special department for the conservation of natural resources of environmental quality. Large cities or counties with a parks department may, on a limited basis, offer jobs for the wildlife biologist. Independent wildlife preservation societies, sanctuaries, rehabilitation centers, and game preserves also employ wildlife biologists.

What Wildlife Biologists Do

What do wildlife biologists do? They are hired primarily to study habitat, heritage, and the survival needs of birds, animals, and other living organisms. They study effects of relationships between species and the effects of pollutants and pesticides on these species. Wildlife biologists also keep track of animals, studying their migration habits, locations, and distribution. They have to study animals' diets and where they find their food, investigate how pollution affects their lives, and generally try to save species from extinction.

Research Biologists

Whenever there is a variation in the natural environment, caused by such things as land developments, temperature alterations, or swamp drainage, natural habitats will change and have an impact on animal and plant life. Research biologists are concerned with fish and wildlife population, plant and animal interactions, and animal habitat requirements, especially regarding nutritional needs. Environmental impact statements often have to be prepared to determine whether certain development programs should be attempted if animal and plant life will be destroyed or disrupted. Refuge managers are primarily concerned with the protection and preservation of both indigenous and migratory fish and wildlife and for setting policy for fishing and hunting.

Fish Biologists

As part of wildlife management, you may choose to become a fish biologist. You would find jobs in a natural setting, such as a park or forest or hatchery. A large part of your work would be to preserve fish habitats by testing water for pollutants. You would spend about half of your time on a boat where you would calculate water volume and collect fish samples and other organic materials. Based on this study, you could then estimate the fish supply for any given lake and plan accordingly.

Marine Biologists

As a biologist, you may decide to work exclusively with organisms found in water rather than those found on land. You would be called a marine or aquatic biologist, and you would study plankton, mussels, and snails, among others. Although some of your work would be done in the laboratory, you would have to collect actual samples from the water in order to study their salt content, acidity, and oxygen level. You would be working with organisms in rivers, lakes, and oceans and would often have to dive into the water in order to gather needed materials to be analyzed.

Because of these on-site investigations, aquatic biologists are often called on to advise and make recommendations on environmental matters to other environmental specialists. These may include engineers, pest control specialists, and water pollution analysts or inspectors.

Marine biologists may also work in conjunction with marine chemists, whose primary task is to study the organic composition of the ocean. They study changing chemical reactions affecting the food chain as well as the amount of carbon dioxide that is in the ocean. Marine biologists also investigate human waste to see how it affects sea life. As a marine biologist, you may also work with geologists, engineers, and oceanographers as well as a variety of technicians.

Oceanographers

Oceanographers are scientists who study tides, currents, and sea level and how climate is affected by these elements. They survey, analyze, and interpret oceanic phenomena. In the future, oceanographers may be able to apply physics, chemistry, geology, and biology to all phases of the global environment.

As a biologist who wants to study the ocean, you would probably be stationed on a research vessel investigating ocean organisms to find out their distribution patterns, behaviors, and adaptation methods to such factors as temperature, light, and food. You may then be able to apply this research to marine policy as it relates to pollution and waste disposal.

Sometimes natural disasters, such as oil spills or man-made waste or sewage, will cause death to thousands of fish at one time. Biologists will then be called in to investigate the cause and make recommendations for the future.

Or you may decide to work in a hatchery, where you will decide which fish should be raised and which equipment will be needed to raise them. Then you will see to it that these fish are allocated to the appropriate lakes. Working closely with you will be the fish culturist, who carries out the daily operations of the hatchery. Culturists often collect and identify fish, take responsibility for constructing ponds, maintain equipment, and supervise distribution of fish to the lakes and reservoirs where they are needed.

Oceanographers find jobs in teaching, consulting, industry, and with the federal government. With a bachelor's degree, you could become a technician or research assistant. Industry and government generally require a master's degree, and if you want to teach, you'll need a Ph.D.

Botanists

Biologists may also choose to work with plants and are called botanists. Botanists work in parks and forests, on farms, and in laboratories. Plant physiologists work specifically on the effects of pesticides on plant life. Some of their work is done in laboratories, conferring with other scientists and testifying at public hearings.

Biotechnologists

A new field is emerging which integrates traditional disciplines, such as biochemistry, microbiology, chemistry, and chemical engineering. It is known as biotechnology, and it attempts to apply new techniques to old practices in order to help cure disease, control pollution, yield better crops, and produce nutritionally improved foods. Agricultural and pharmaceutical companies as well as government agencies employ biotechnologists. Those biotechnologists working specifically toward environment or crop improvement may have to do fieldwork at landfills or at agricultural sites. Others may work almost exclusively in laboratories.

Zoological Careers

Most of us have been to the zoo at one time or another. Maybe we went because the only animals we had ever seen were cats, dogs, an occasional cow or horse, maybe some robins or sparrows. But zebras, giraffes, elephants, or baboons? Hardly likely. The exotic animals, birds, and snakes from Asia, South America, and Africa were there to entertain and amuse us. It was a great place to go with the family on a summer Sunday. Besides, we could usually get some cotton candy, popcorn, and ice cream all in one day.

At one time, all the animals were in cages, usually only with members of their own species. Sometimes the architecture would not allow you to see the animals you came to view.

But the purpose and function of the zoo has changed in the last 50 years—often for environmental reasons. Many natural habitats have been destroyed because of land development and pollution, and whole species have become endangered, if not extinct. Modern zoos are trying to recreate natural environments and conserve species by duplicating as closely as possible flora and fauna of their habitat and breeding in captivity those animals that are endangered. They are then often released to special reserves or forests.

Typically, today's zoo will have a bird house, a monkey house, and a great ape house. Other areas will house hoofed animals, elephants, giraffes, lions, tigers, sea lions, beavers, bears, and otters. Amphibians, reptiles, birds, and invertebrates are also often included. Habitats such as wetlands, trails, creeks, and small forests are also found in zoos. Most zoos also have educational and ecological exhibits and research and breeding facilities.

Since more and more zoological parks are becoming "bioparks," much of the work is done outside with the animals. Biologists, botanists, ecologists, ornithologists, mammalogists, physiologists, and zoologists work together to try to create an environment that might come close to that which we have almost destroyed.

Zoologists

Those of you who wish to work for the conservation, protection, and preservation of individual animals and whole species may choose to become zoologists. Zoologists of today may also be working toward the so-called biological park of the future where more plants, water animals, and other scientific innovations will further transform the focus of the zoological park.

The zoologist has the responsibility of planning the future of the collection, maintaining records, and obtaining necessary permits and licenses. Research zoologists are more involved with the ecology and behavior of the animals and seek ways to improve their care. Research may also involve reproduction and breeding in captivity.

Zookeepers

Zookeepers' responsibilities revolve around maintaining and cleaning animal habitats and feeding the animals. Zookeepers also have to be well informed on animal behavior, habitat, breeding, and hygiene. They often are called on to answer visitors' questions about the various animals in the zoo. They may also work on independent projects in their field. They can become biological technicians if they specialize in a specific area of expertise.

Other Positions

If you choose to work in an outside job in a zoological park, you could work as a gardener, tree worker, or maintenance worker. These workers are also needed in parks, science centers, and aquariums.

Ecological Careers

Of all the career opportunities we have looked at so far, that of the ecologist is the one that brings together the study of all natural systems—earth, air, water, plants, and animals. Connections between living organisms and effects of their interactions are ecologists' concerns. Much of the ecologist's work is done outside—on the ocean, in a rain forest, in an urban setting. The balance of nature, wherever it occurs, is what you will investigate and analyze.

Aquatic Ecologists

Aquatic ecologists observe plant and animal life in or near natural bodies of water. Many factors affect marine life, including the water's temperature, toxic level, acidity, light, and oxygen. Whether you work with saltwater or freshwater, your main concern will be how plants and animals live in that particular environment. You will also be able to foresee what can alter the ecological balance of all life forms in water.

Plant Ecologists

Plant ecologists apply many of the same principles to plant life and those factors, such as temperature, rainfall, soil content, and elevation, that affect the growing seed. The reproductive life of plants as well as their population patterns and economic worth are part of the plant ecologist's job. As a plant ecologist, you would be working with other professionals whose careers depend on an understanding of plants, such as agricultural scientists, foresters, rangers, and horticulturists.

Animal Ecology

If you prefer to build your career around the interactions of animals with their environment, you will want to explore the field of animal ecology. These ecologists study not only the present status of animals and their environment but also their origin and history. The study of habitat and diseases as well as geographical location is also a part of the work of the animal ecologist.

Animal ecologists also try to prevent animal extinction by studying, for example, the effects of pesticides on animal populations. Pesticides that are harmful to animals often have the same effects on humans, so that studying their diseases may be very helpful to human and plant life.

All ecologists perform the major portion of their work outdoors—on the ocean, in forests, mountains, cities, and farms.

That means that they work in all climates throughout the year. They may then be called upon to work in the laboratory to analyze data and write reports and recommendations based on their study.

Getting Started in Biology Careers

Now, how do you get started in this field? First, you probably have to be interested in science courses in high school. Advanced biology, chemistry, and physics courses are recommended as well as math, English, and computer science. While you are still in high school, it is a good idea to decide which career path appeals to you and choose a college that will fulfill the requirements of your choice. At this time, it may also be good to take a cold, hard look at employment possibilities to help you make the right decision.

Because of our highly technological society, the nature lover with the highest degree of education will probably get the best job. However, if you have just a high school diploma, you could get a job as a greenhouse aide, animal care assistant, landscape gardener, or tree worker. With two years of college or some technical training, you could become a technician or warden. Biologists, botanists, zoologists, biotechnologists, and ecologists, however, should have at least a bachelor's degree. For some careers, or for advancement in your career track, a master's degree or Ph.D. is essential.

It is important for you to know that, although you may do most of your work in the great outdoors, you may also be called on to write reports and recommendations, to work with others on team projects, and occasionally to communicate directly with the public. For example, you may have to testify at public hearings or make public decisions based on your knowledge or your fieldwork. A well-rounded education will prepare you for all these eventualities and provide expanded opportunities for advancement.

Educational Qualifications for Wildlife, Fishing, and Research Biologists

As a wildlife biologist, fishing biologist, research biologist, or refuge manager, you would more than likely be employed by the government, either state or federal. Some independent agencies may also have limited opportunities.

The primary federal employer of biologists is the Fish and Wildlife Service of the Department of the Interior. Its wildlife biologists need 30 semester hours in biology. This includes nine hours in subjects relating to wildlife. In addition, they need 12 hours in zoology and 9 hours in botany.

Fishery biologists for the Fish and Wildlife Service also need 30 semester hours of biology. This includes six semester hours in aquatic-related subjects and 12 semester hours in animal science. Research biologists have to have at least a bachelor's degree in biology, zoology, or aquatic science, plus 15 semester hours in any physical science or mathematics. Managerial positions require only nine semester hours of zoology and six in wildlife subjects. Other federal employers of biologists are the Environmental Protection Agency, the National Park Service, and the Forest Service.

The certification program of the Wildlife Society, an independent organization, requires a bachelor's degree with 36 semester hours in the biological sciences, including principles of wildlife management, biology, ornithology, mammalogy, plant or animal ecology, zoology, genetics, physiology, anatomy, and taxonomy.

Nine semester hours are required in the physical sciences, such as chemistry, physics, or geology, and nine in quantitative sciences, such as calculus, statistics, computer science, or biometry. Also necessary are courses in the humanities, social sciences, communications, policy, administration, and law.

Another private agency, the Wildlife Habitat Enhancement Council, employs a director of field operations and wildlife biologist who work in the office as well as outdoors. Educational requirements for the director's position include a bachelor's degree in wildlife management/biology/zoology. A person with a higher degree would be preferred. This position demands highly developed communication skills, supervisory skills, knowledge of environmental laws, and an ability to manage data systems. The wildlife biologist must have a bachelor's degree in wildlife biology or a related field, computer skills, analytical skills, and public relations and communication skills.

Every state has a conservation agency that employs biologists. The titles of these departments vary from state to state, but they all sound similar: wildlife and fisheries commission, department of natural resources, game and fish commission, or wildlife resources commission. They are usually located in the state capital.

Educational and training requirements will vary somewhat from state to state, but, generally speaking, the more education and training you have, the better career opportunities you will have. The individual department in your state will provide you with all the necessary information that you will need to pursue a career with it. In Canada, you should contact the Canadian Wildlife Service.

If you really don't know which area of specialization you prefer by the time you are an undergraduate, you should take the required courses in a broadly based program of communications skills, humanities, foreign language, social sciences, at least introductory courses in the physical and quantitative sciences, and mathematics. You can then concentrate on more advanced study in a specific area in graduate school.

While you are in high school or college, it is a good idea to do volunteer work at your local anticruelty society, zoo, park, nature reserve, or state park or forest. The Fish and Wildlife Service offers an extensive volunteer program at fish hatcheries, wildlife refuges, and research stations throughout the United States. There are more than 400 centers located in eight regions..

As a volunteer, you may assist in taking population censuses, work on habitat construction and maintenance, or feed and care for animals. Different stations have different needs, and some work may be seasonal. It is also probably more convenient for you to apply for volunteer work near your home since housing is not usually provided. You don't have to have any special skills to volunteer because you will receive on-the-job training. Special skills are, however, always welcome.

Educational Qualifications for Aquatic and Marine Biologists

If you choose to become an aquatic or marine biologist, the educational requirements may vary somewhat, but a well-rounded education and lots of it will be the best way to open the door of opportunity. In high school, you should take your basic science courses, mathematics, English, computer science, and a foreign language. If possible, take advanced biology courses at this time, too.

By the time you get to college, you may be able to get a degree in marine science, with the requirement that you take on a second major, which will require another year in school. You may choose to take a broader scientific curriculum and attend summer sessions with a group like the Sea Education Association in Massachusetts. If you want to be more than a technician or research assistant, you will choose to attend graduate school. Your career counselor should be able to guide you in the selection of a graduate program suited to your needs. Some directories that may be helpful to you are also available in college and public libraries, including *Curricula in the Atmospheric, Oceanic and Related Sciences* and *Sourcebook of Colleges and Universities.*

You might also want to participate in science fairs and competitions while you're in school or do volunteer work in a local aquarium or tropiquarium during school breaks. The Student Conservation Association, Inc., in New Hampshire, offers volunteer work during summer vacations, too.

You might also have branches of national conservation societies in your community, such as Greenpeace, Sierra Club, or Sea Shepherd, where you can work during breaks or summer vacations. A summer camp in Florida, Sea Camp, has a strong marine biology specialization. If you are really interested in marine biology, you may also use your summer vacations to learn how to swim, boat, and dive. After that, you may want to work as a volunteer in an underwater research facility.

Educational Qualifications for Botanists

Botanists should also follow a solid science curriculum in high school, with a variety of science and math courses. Strong communications and computer science skills should be developed, and any kind of related extracurricular activities that will round out your development are often required. Emphasis in college will be on botany, but environmental courses, physiology, biology, agriculture, and soil sciences will also be important for your career. A strong liberal arts base and any kind of work in the laboratory or in the field will be a plus.

Educational Qualifications for Biotechnologists

Since biotechnology integrates scientific disciplines, including biochemistry and physiology, you will have to have a strong background in all sciences. Since this is a comparatively new field, too, you will be in a very good position for a career with advanced science courses in college and a master's degree for good measure.

Educational Qualifications for Zoologists

A career as a zoologist will require a bachelor's degree, preferably in zoology, animal sciences, or biology. A zookeeper usually needs a high school diploma, but some college experience or animal care work would put you in a better position for employment. A college degree is preferred.

Educational Qualifications for Ecologists

The requirements for ecologists are much the same as for any other biologist. A college degree is essential, with an emphasis on biology. But you should also study chemistry and physics, math, statistics, and computer science. Depending on which branch of ecology you choose, consider taking geology, oceanography, soil science, physiology, or morphology. Social sciences, communication skills, and anthropology should round out your education.

As an ecologist, your work area may be in a forest or on a farm, on the ocean or in the mountains. You may also work in the city. So you may want to do some volunteer work in your local park or state facility, go on field trips, do research projects, or serve as an intern when you're in high school or college.

Where to Find the Jobs

As we have seen, the federal government is a major employer of environmental workers, but you will also find jobs at the state, county, and municipal level of government. Corporations are also becoming more and more involved in environmental impact regulations and are therefore hiring biologists to help them comply with government regulations. Independent grass-roots and nonprofit organizations hire biologists only on a limited basis but should be looked into for possible career opportunities.

Obtaining a Federal Job

If you decide to work for the federal government, you will have to be evaluated by the Office of Personnel Management (OPM) in any Federal Job Information Center. The OPM not only maintains a listing of candidates but also refers them to government agencies. Federal Job Centers are usually found in large cities listed in the phone book under "U.S. Government." You should ask for the pamphlet "Working for the USA" for further information.

In order to apply for a federal job, you have to file the following:

1. Standard Form 171

2. OPM Form 1170/17 or send college transcript

3. Occupational Supplement for Biological Sciences Positions, Form B (OPM Form 1203-1)

4. SF-15 Claim for 10-Point Veteran Preference, if it applies

Since regulations and salaries change periodically, it's a good idea to inquire first before sending anything. Currently you should send all this information to: Office of Personnel Management, Staffing Service Center Examining Office, P.O. Box 9025, Macon, GA 31297-4599. You may also indicate at this time in which geographic area of the country you would prefer to work.

Salary Outlook

Salaries for the federal government are set at so-called "GS" levels, listed on the General Schedule Pay Scale that you can get from your local OPM. So, for instance, if you were classified as a biologist at a GS-5 level, you would have to have at least a bachelor's degree in biology or related subject from an accredited institution. Or you may qualify with a combination of college courses and work experience. At the GS-5 level, the salary range is $16,973–$22,067 a year.

Further education and/or work experience may then advance you to the GS-7 level, where your annual salary range would be $21,023–$27,332. According to the latest pay schedule, there are 18 GS levels available, the highest being paid $97,317 annually. But it would probably take a lot of years, education, and work experience to achieve that salary level!

Obtaining a State Job

Many states have rather stringent requirements for employment, including physical health, education, and experience. Be sure to check with your state agency for all those details before you apply. Government jobs are usually fairly stable, and the career track is clearly spelled out for you. On the other hand, they are also very competitive, so your education and training are very important.

Salary Outlook

State governments' salaries and requirements will vary. For example, in 1990 a game and fish commission biologist II in Arkansas had an annual starting salary of $18,200, but a biologist I started at $16,068. In North Carolina, a biologist I salary range was $21,566–$34,440 per year. A fisheries biologist was the same. The top annual salary for a senior wildlife biologist in New York was $65,000.

Obtaining a Private-Sector Job

Recruiting for many private-sector jobs starts with advertisements in the local newspaper or the newsletter or a professional organization. The Job Seeker, published twice a month in Warrens, Wisconsin, is a listing of vacancies in natural resource and environmental positions throughout the country. It is available to universities, organizations, corporations, and individuals. You can receive a free issue upon request.

Organizations with branches throughout the country, such as Greenpeace, might advertise in the Wall Street Journal, the New York Times, or other appropriate national publications. Positions available at their headquarters city are advertised in the local newspaper. The Sierra Club also has a JOBLINE telephone number (415-978-9085) in San Francisco. Its salary and benefits package is competitive, and tuition reimbursement is possible.

Corporations generally require the same educational and work experience as most government and independent agencies, but the salaries may be higher. They advertise in both local and national newspapers and through professional organizations. The various professional organizations or your career counselor at school may help you decided what a competitive salary might be according to your education and work experience, including internship and volunteer work.

Salary Outlook

Salary ranges will also vary within the private sector of employment. For example, a 1990 membership survey of the National Association of Environmental Professionals yielded the following profile:

1. A typical member earns from $41,000 to $50,000 annually with 12 years' experience.

2. A majority (72 percent) of members have a graduate degree, usually an M.S.

Those who had worked an average of four years had a salary range of $10,000–$20,000 yearly; an average of 22 years, $91,000–$100,000. Twenty-five percent of the respondents were scientists/engineers, including biologists.

The Center for Holistic Resource Management in New Mexico is a small organization with only 10 full-time employees. Field trainees need a background in environmental science, community development, and adult education. The salaries, including administrative, range from $20,000–$60,000 annually.

The Wildlife Habitat Enhancement Council employs a director of field programs at a salary range of $35,000–$50,000 annually and a wildlife biologist with a salary range of $20,000–$35,000. The director must have at least a B.S. in wildlife management, wildlife biology, or zoology. Related work experience and graduate work are preferred. The biologist should have a B.S. in wildlife biology in addition to computer skills, an understanding of environmental issues, and good communication skills.

Choosing a Biology Career

So if you decide that your love of nature will lead you to the field of biology, whether as an aquatic, wildlife, or fisheries biologist, an ecologist or biotechnologist, your opportunities for employment are very favorable over the next several years. This is especially true in the fields of waste disposal, pollution, and disease control. Since our society is growing older, any biological problems associated with aging will have to be studied, along with associated diseases, drugs, and medicines.

If you want to become a biologist, you will have to take some very definite steps in preparing for your career. Careful thought concerning where you want to work, in which area of the biological sciences, and for whom you want to work will affect your decision. The choices are wide and various, and only you can set the limits of your achievement.

You already know of the environmental problems with water, air, and land. It is now up to you to do something lasting to preserve these natural resources that you love so much.

For Further Information

American Institute of Biological Sciences, 730 11th Street, NW, Washington, DC 20001-4584

American Society of Biochemistry and Molecular Biology, Charles C. Hancock, Executive Director, 9650 Rockville Pike, Bethesda, MD 20814

American Society of Zoologists, 104 Sirius Circle, Thousand Oaks, CA 91360

BioSciences Information Service, Donald J. Castagna, Controller, 2100 Arch Street, Philadelphia, PA 19103-1399

Botanical Society of America, Dr. David Dilcher, Department of Biology, Jordan Hall, Indiana University, Bloomington, IN 17405

American Association of Zoological Parks and Aquariums, Oglebay Park, Wheeling, WV 26003-1698

National Zoological Park, Smithsonian Institution, Washington, DC 20008

Society of Protozoologists, Jerome J. Paulin, Department of Zoology, University of Georgia, Athens, GA 30602

American Association of Zoo Keepers, National Headquarters, 635 Gage Boulevard, Topeka, KS 66606

Torrey Botanical Club. New York Botanical Garden, Bronx, NY 10458

"Careers in Botany," Botanical Society of America, c/o Gregory Anderson, 75 North Eagleville Road, U-43 University of Connecticut, Storrs, CT 06268

The Ecological Society of America, Public Affairs Office, 9650 Rockville Pike, Bethesda, MD 20814

Office of Opportunities in Sciences, 1776 Massachusetts Avenue, NW, Washington, DC 20036

Organization of Biological Field Stations, Dr. Richard W. Coles, Tyson Research Center, P.O. Box 258, Eureka, MO 63025

The Wildlife Society, 5410 Grosvenor Lane, Bethesda, MD 20814

American Fisheries Society, 5410 Grosvenor Lane, Bethesda, MD 20814

U.S. Fish and Wildlife Service, Publications Unit, U.S. Department of the Interior, Mail Stop 725, ArlSq, 18th and C Streets, NW, Washington, DC 20240

National Park Service, Interior Building, P.O. Box 37127, Washington, DC 20013-7127

U.S. Environmental Protection Agency, Personnel Management Division (PM-212), Washington, DC 20460

U.S. Department of Commerce, National Marine Fishery Service, Personnel Office, 1335 East West Highway, Silver Spring, MD 20910 ATTN: OA211FISH

National Oceanic and Atmospheric Administration (NOAA), Rockville, MD 20852

Society for Marine Mammalogy, c/o Robert Brownell, Jr., U.S. Fish and Wildlife Service, P.O. Box 70, San Simeon, CA 93452

American Society of Biological Chemists, 9650 Rockville Pike, Bethesda, MD 20814

Sea Education Association, P.O. Box 6, Woods Hole, MA 02543

Sea Camp, Route 3, Box 170, Big Pine Key, FL 33043

Center for Marine Conservation, Inc., 1725 DeSales Street, NW, Suite 500, Washington, DC 20036

The Job Seeker, Route 2, Box 16, Warrens, WI 54666

Job Scan, Student Conservation Association, P.O. Box 550, Charlestown, NH 03603

Canadian Wildlife Service, Place Vincent Massey, Ottawa, Ontario K1A 0E7 Canada

"Biological Scientists, Wildlife Management, Fisheries Scientists, Oceanographers, Zoologists." Chronicle Guidance Publications, Aurora Street, P.O. Box 1190, Moravia, NY 13118-1190

Wildlife Habitat Enhancement Council, 1010 Wayne Avenue, Suite 1240, Silver Spring, MD 20910

Sierra Club, 730 Polk Street, San Francisco, CA 94109

Center for Holistic Resource Management, 5820 Fourth Street, NW, Albuquerque, NM 87107

National Association of Environmental Professionals, P.O. Box 15210, Alexandria, VA 22390-0210

American Geophysical Union, 2000 Florida Avenue, NW, Washington, DC 20009

Scripps Institution of Oceanography of the University of California, La Jolla, CA 92093

Woods Hole Oceanographic Institution, Woods Hole, MA 02543

CHAPTER THREE

Careers in the Agricultural Sciences

T he field of agriculture offers a wide variety of career opportunities for nature lovers with different specializations and levels of education. As we know, nutritious and safe foods are at the heart of all life. Chemical pollutants, pesticides, and hazardous underground waste material are some of the threats to the growth of healthy, nutritional food.

The fact that the United States is a country with abundant food supplies is not an accident. Many people supply technical and scientific knowledge to the farming community, not only to assure adequate amounts of food for home use and export but also to guarantee the quality of that food. These scientists must also work within strict environmental standards.

The Importance of Agronomists

The basic field of plants and soil study is called agronomy. When applied to farming, it becomes a crop science, which encompasses cell biology, physiology, genetics, and breeding. Crop scientists are also concerned with producing seeds of high quality. Those areas involved with the soil sciences include soil physics, chemistry, and microbiology as they relate to plants.

The study of crops and soil is extremely important, not only for the continued production of high-quality food for our country but also to work toward lessening the problems of worldwide hunger for all people. This is one of many challenges for today's agronomists.

As we are seeing, in order to protect the environment from further deterioration and to assure continued quality of the food chain, scientists, technicians, researchers, and field workers have to work together and share information with members of different teams, sometimes in different parts of the world. So it is with agronomists, who must share information with chemists, physicists, mathematicians, biologists, geologists, and animal scientists.

What Agronomists Do

Much of the effort of today's agronomists is applied to reducing environmental pollution. Some agronomists may be primarily concerned with how pesticides react in the soil and groundwater. They investigate how long it takes for them to break down and how toxic the process will be. Others concentrate on the dumping of waste material into the soil.

Other agronomists, who want to work more closely with farming problems, work at agricultural extension services. These are usually located at land-grant universities, where agronomists work with specific problems of farmers and help them to manage their farms better.

The federal government also employs agronomists in the Soil Conservation Service and the Forest Service. These agronomists' concerns are primarily with farmers and ranchers and how they can manage their land effectively and conserve the soil at the same time.

Many agronomists are increasingly becoming farmers and ranchers themselves. Their college or university education is actually utilized on their own crops and soil to make a living.

Since agronomists are involved in the vital work of crop production and soil conservation, their work is needed all over the world. Universities, government agencies, and various foundations, as well as agriculture-related businesses with branches in foreign countries, need the services of agronomists to help solve the nutritional needs of developing nations throughout the world. So if you are a person with a bit of wanderlust, you may consider agronomy as a career.

Educational Requirements

Now that your curiosity has been aroused, you might ask yourself how you might become an agronomist. In high school, you should study the basic sciences, including biology, chemistry, math, and physics. English is required, and foreign languages are recommended if you see yourself in a faraway place in the future.

By the time you get to college, the following courses are highly recommended: geology, botany, microbiology, genetics, plant physiology, soil chemistry, plant pathology, entomology, biochemistry, and meteorology. With the Bachelor of Science degree, you could be a farmer, agricultural agent, or soil conservationist.

If you decide to get a master's degree, you will find more career opportunities available, both in research and agricultural extension programs. Both governmental and private-sector agencies and organizations need highly skilled and educated professionals now and in the future as the need for environmentally safe crops and "clean" soil continues.

With your B.S. in agronomy, you may choose to apply to the American Registry of Certified Professionals in Agronomy, Crops, and Soils (ARCPACS). The registry holds members to a code of ethics and establishes standards for their practice of agronomy. To qualify, you must have a certain combination of education and work experience. Or you can apply for the professional-in-training status.

Certification by the ARCPACS is becoming more and more the norm for hiring by most employers. You may qualify for certification in the following categories: agronomist, crop scientist, crop specialist, soil scientist, soil specialist, or soil classifier. As a soil scientist, you may specialize as a soil classifier or soil erosion and sediment control specialist.

Salary Outlook

Although salaries vary from location to location and agency to agency, we can generalize to this extent: in 1989, agronomy students with a bachelor's degree had a starting salary range from $19,470 to $23,100 a year. With a master's degree, you could earn from $32,000 to $45,000.

Other Types of Agriculture Careers
Agricultural Pest Control Specialists

If you are a nature lover interested in working on agricultural problems, but you don't want to devote as much time to your education as an agronomist, you may consider the career of agricultural pest control specialist. On the job, you would take samples of crops and inspect them for signs of dangerous organisms or harmful insect infestation. You would be able to assist in proposing effective methods of disease prevention or using predators to eradicate the offending pests.

The specialist often trains and coordinates crews of workers who are brought in to spray pesticides. They must learn to operate the equipment and applicators. At this level, the specialist also has to use management skills to make assignments, train workers, evaluate them, and be responsible for the working order of all equipment.

Pest control specialists are responsible for working with farmers and governmental agencies. They may work on land or occasionally from airplanes, where they will apply pesticides from the air.

To be hired as a trainee, you should have two years of full-time agricultural work experience. Six months of these two years should be in agricultural pest control work. However, you may substitute $1^{1}/_{2}$ years of college coursework for the agricultural work experience. As a pest control specialist, you will have to be knowledgeable in surveying and controlling pests as well as in the current laws and regulations regarding pesticides.

Your prospects for employment as a pest control specialist are quite good, primarily with state and federal government agencies. Some states now require licensing, so be sure to check with your state's licensing board. In order to be licensed, it will be necessary to have a college degree in many states, but you will have to keep up with the changing educational standards for licensing.

Pest Control Helpers

Those of you who may want to enter the pest control field before committing your time to a great deal of education may want to start out as a pest control helper. As a helper, you would assist in controlling rodents in agricultural fields and buildings. You might set traps, dig out harmful weeds, burn or spray, and try to identify likely places of infestation.

To become a pest control helper, you will have to be healthy and strong, dexterous and agile. But there are no educational standards or work experience requirements for the job. You may then advance, with some work experience, to the title of pest exterminator.

Pest Exterminators

Pest exterminators are employed by private industry and are found in the city and on the farm. Pests can infest not only crops but also buildings and other farm facilities and even farm animals. After initial inspections, exterminators make recommendations for treatment. Since termites are often the major culprits in any wooden structure, inspectors and helpers repair damage to both the structure and the soil.

Much of your work as a pest exterminator will be outdoors in all kinds of weather conditions. It will be strenuous and may involve bending, crawling, climbing, and lifting. You will have to be physically strong and have stamina to do this kind of work.

Although there are no educational requirements for this work, some states require licensing. You will have to know about rules and regulations concerning pesticides, dangerous pests, and extermination and prevention methods. You generally become an exterminator by receiving on-the-job training as a helper.

Entomologists

Entomologists are divided into two categories: systematic and economic. Both work with insects. Systematic entomologists work in laboratories; economic, in the field. These entomologists determine the geographical range of insects through surveys, and then their economic impact is evaluated.

You can become an entomologist with a college degree with emphasis on entomology and the zoological sciences. You must know how to classify major pests and how to identify and control them. You should also be familiar with horticulture, plant relationships, and plant pests as they relate to agriculture.

Entomology Field Assistants

Working alongside entomologists are entomology field assistants, who aid in trapping, fumigating, and spraying insects. They also supervise work crews and keep records. Often their work includes writing reports about their fieldwork.

With some work experience, assistants can survey infestations, track insect populations, evaluate control programs, and measure results. As with most environmental workers, field assistants are called upon to work with other specialists and technicians in government agencies and agriculture-related businesses.

You will need at least two years of agriculture-related work to obtain an entry-level position as an entomology field assistant. Some of this experience should include work on insect control projects. You will have to know about pest control methods and equipment, which may include spray guns and turbine blowers. Your career will probably be with local and state government agencies, and you can work your way up with additional experience.

Plant Physiologists

Plant physiologists divide their work between the field and the laboratory. They conduct research on pesticides and then apply it to agricultural crops and plants. Plant physiologists also investigate the toxicity of pesticides and chemicals that are applied to agriculture.

If you work for the government, you may advise manufacturers as to the safety of new pesticides before they are labeled. Or you may have to testify at public hearings or in court as an expert witness. As with other scientists working with the natural environment, you may work with other scientists, technicians, agriculture extension service workers, and various other professionals.

To be a plant physiologist, you have to have a college degree. You should study all the biological sciences with a major in plant physiology. You would then be qualified for an entry-level position if you have no work experience. The more work experience and education you have, the better chance you will have for increased responsibilities and salary. Your best career opportunities are now with state and local government.

The Pesticide Controversy

The use of pesticides has, of course, caused a great deal of controversy in recent years. Many that have been used in the past are considered too toxic for use now. They have, therefore, been banned. Some that are now used are being challenged by independent organizations as being carcinogenic or too toxic for use in the food chain. Federal, state, and local governments have set up regulatory agencies for toxins and pesticides, and private organizations serve a vital watchdog function to those agencies to protect the environment and plant, animal, and human life.

The Federal Insecticide, Fungicide, and Rodenticide Act of 1947 was amended in 1972 and revised in 1978. Essentially it provides for federal control over the application of pesticides and regulation of the marketing of these products. It has become apparent in recent years that protection of the environment is everybody's job and that particular attention has to be paid to any substance used on crops or in the soil that holds the crops.

For instance, a recent U.S. Geological Survey study found that pesticides commonly used on crops in Illinois are getting into the rainwater by evaporating into the clouds. As these clouds move, the polluted rain then may fall in any location. The pesticides in question are atrazine, alachlor, and metolachlor. In some places where the rainwater has fallen, the concentration of pesticides has exceeded the U.S. Environmental Protection Agency (EPA) standards. This may be why the now-banned DDT can still be found all over the world. This also demonstrates that environmental concerns are global and must be tackled both locally and globally. Government, industry, and private associations must continually monitor the natural environment and make their reports known to the public for its input.

The EPA acknowledges that the use of pesticides is a two-edged sword. Some pesticides have actually reduced crop damage; others have saved lives by controlling insects that carry diseases. They have helped to preserve forests and parks and have stopped fruit from dropping before it is ripe. They can also retard fungicidal growth.

But whenever they stay in the environment and spread beyond the area where they are intended to be of use, they may invade the food we eat, the air we breathe, and the land that sustains the food. They become dangerous and harmful. They may even be affecting the reproductive cycle of certain birds and the ability of species to survive.

Experts in agricultural entomology estimate that farmers have reduced their use of pesticides by 22 percent for soybeans and 16 percent for corn in Illinois alone. The trend for farmers may be to reduce the use of pesticides in general because they realize some of the dangers. It has also been estimated that the use of herbicides could be reduced by as much as 50 percent if farmers would alternate rows with weed-smothering crops or apply weed killer only where needed instead of on every crop.

If you decide to become a farmer or pest control specialist, you must be very careful when reading labels and exercise care in the use of chemicals that affect the food chain, soil, water, or air.

Federal Agencies

The federal agencies set up to monitor toxic substances are the Environmental Protection Agency (EPA), the Food and Drug Administration (FDA), the Occupational Health and Safety Administration (OSHA), and the Consumer Product Safety Commission (CPSC). The EPA is primarily responsible for the protection of the environment from pesticides.

Agricultural Scientists

The work of agricultural scientists and technicians is with food production and processing. They may test crops for quality and yield, or they may test plants and animals for resistance to insects and disease. In so doing, they have to monitor experiments and evaluate results. Most of their work is done outdoors and is often dangerous since they may be working with toxic substances or diseased organisms.

Agricultural science biologists need a bachelor's degree with a biological science major. You will have to take at least 10 semester hours in plant biology and 10 in vertebrate biology. In addition, you will have to be knowledgeable in botany, zoology, mammalogy; botanical and zoological classification; pest control methods; and agriculture-related pest problems.

You may also want to work in nurseries or seed fields where you'll study insects and plants and serve as consultant to agriculture businesses. Or you could work at border control stations, inspecting and advising on regulations relating to agricultural imports and exports. This can occur at the borders between states, counties, and countries.

Agricultural scientists are needed throughout the world, but here in the United States you might want to contact the U. S. Department of Agriculture for employment opportunities. State and local governments are also good sources for jobs as well as agricultural experiment stations and agribusiness.

Agricultural scientists could start at annual salaries of $20,220 or more with some experience. Starting salaries decrease with no experience. Your job prospects are quite good for the next several years.

Veterinarians

Veterinarians are employed by the U.S. Department of Agriculture and the U.S. Food and Drug Administration. In some cases, when they are working in the agricultural sciences, they try to improve breeding and management of livestock or study diseases and insects that affect farm animals, including poultry. Agriculture experiment stations at state universities also employ agricultural veterinarians.

The demand for veterinarians who specialize in the public health sector, which includes agriculture, seems to be growing because there is an increasing animal census and because breeding methods have improved. Salaries vary according to the location of a practice and work experience. Your education will include a degree in veterinary medicine (DVM) from an accredited college. The emphasis will be on biological and physical sciences, mathematics, and chemistry. Later you will take pathology, applied anatomy, clinical medicine, pharmacology, microbiology, and surgery. Veterinarians should be well versed in English, social sciences, and the humanities. You will also have laboratory and clinical work in addition to classroom lecture and discussion.

If you decide to become a veterinarian specializing in agricultural services, you will have to have many years of schooling and be dedicated to the improvement of the total environment—animal, plant, and human life—because of the close interrelationships at this level. Animals may get diseased because they have eaten tainted or polluted food, and that disease, in turn, can be transmitted to humans who eat the animal. So the veterinarian who works on the farm eventually will have an effect on the rural, suburban, and urban population of living things. Other scientists involved with agriculture are the animal physiologist, who studies the physiology of livestock, and the animal scientist, who specializes in the breeding and marketing of farm animals and in disease control of those animals.

Chemists

If your specialty is chemistry, you can also become involved in agriculture. Because of the many pollutants in the environment, organic, inorganic, analytical, and physical chemists are needed to work in connection with governmental agencies and other agricultural scientists. You will probably divide your work between the field and the laboratory, primarily helping to enforce the laws that ensure safety in the manufacture of chemicals used in agriculture. In the laboratory, you will examine pesticides, analyze them, and see if they are toxic. Then you will determine under which conditions and dosages they pollute or contaminate. You will have to collect samples in the field and then follow certain scientific procedures to evaluate solutions. In your analysis and evaluation, you will deal with pesticides, fertilizers, residues, and feed. Since your work directly involves public health, you may be called on to present your findings at public hearings and evaluate the environmental impact of pesticides and chemicals.

You will have to have a degree in chemistry or biochemistry. Work experience of one or two years may also may be required for some jobs if you don't have a master's degree or Ph.D. You will find employment with the government or industry. Your job title may be either agricultural chemist or environmental chemist. Salaries vary according to academic degree, work experience, and private- or public-sector employment.

Chemical Technicians

Chemical technicians work alongside chemists in the manufacturing process or on the farm. They should have a background in applied chemistry, mathematics, and basic laboratory equipment. These skills can be acquired at an accredited college or in a two-year program. Junior or community colleges, some trade or technical schools, and four-year colleges will offer you the necessary courses.

You may get further training on the job, but employers are increasingly looking for technicians with a two-year degree rather than unskilled workers who have to be completely trained on the job. Your starting salary will probably range from $14,000–$28,000 a year, with the national average at $20,000.

Biotechnologists

Biotechnologists are also needed in agriculture and pesticide work. Biotechnology applies the disciplines of biochemistry, chemistry, microbiology, and chemical engineering to a wide variety of products and processes. Biotechnologists investigate ways to improve crops through alteration of genes so that plants manufacture their own natural pesticides. They also work on producing plants with more protein, thereby improving their nutritional value.

The Need for Agricultural Professionals

We can now understand, from viewing these career possibilities, that planting food and bringing it to harvest, guaranteeing the health of plants and animals, and using the soil wisely is a very complex operation. Growing plants and animals depend on clean air, suitable soil, nonpolluted water, and nutritional feed and fertilizers. Farming in this country no longer resembles a Norman Rockwell illustration of a nuclear family tilling the soil on their own plot of land that has been passed on from generation to generation. Pollution, advanced technology, agribusiness, and harmful pesticides and chemicals have made dealing with the food chain very complicated. Many farmers have opted for organic methods in order to completely avoid the hazards of applying any pesticide to crop.

In an area as vital as agriculture, it is essential that all scientists and technicians work together with the farmer, rancher, consumer, and government agencies to provide safe food today and improved crops for tomorrow. Our country and the world's population are in great need of good food and an equitable distribution of it.

Highly educated and trained professionals are needed. They should be knowledgeable in their field and should have some familiarity with computers, satellites, and telemetry instruments. Interdisciplinary cooperation and application of mathematics, communication skills, social sciences, critical thinking, and analytical skills will have to be utilized to make it all happen. Laboratory workers will have to share with field workers, chemists with biologists, biotechnologists with agronomists, soil scientists with pest control specialists. Plant and animal physiologists will share information with ecologists and crop specialists; and state, local, and federal agencies will have to enforce laws concerning labeling and use of agricultural products. Consumers will have to be aware of the ramifications of all these processes and demand the safety and nutrition of all foods that are consumed by animals and humans. Creative solutions will have to be found for the problems of world hunger that will take us into the next century.

Agricultural Organizations

Farm Animal Reform Movement

For every government agency or industry involved with agriculture, there are as many independent agencies seeking protection of animals on factory farms and in agribusiness. One such organization is the Farm Animal Reform Movement (FARM). The organization sponsors the annual Great American Meatout, when Americans are urged not to eat meat for one day. By protesting slaughterhouse practices and factory farming of chickens and cattle and supporting the Veal Calf Protection Act of 1990, this group is doing a great deal toward effecting more humane treatment of farm animals.

Humane Farming Association

Another such organization is the Humane Farming Association, known especially for its campaign against factory farming and its effects on the quality of meat that it produces. Its campaign to boycott veal is well known and has consisted of TV commercials, education, and legislation.

Although these organizations may not have many career opportunities, they will provide you with information about the farming industry that you might not get from more traditional agencies.

So the future should be bright, complex, exciting, and rewarding for you if you choose to show your love of nature in the very important field of agriculture. No matter which path you take, education, training, willingness to work with others to come up with solutions, eagerness to learn new techniques, and the ability to devise new strategies will help you find a career. You may work in the private or public sector or buy your own farm or ranch and apply your knowledge and ideas to your own plot of land.

For Further Information

American Society of Agronomy, 677 South Segoe Road, Madison, WI 53711

Crop Society of America, 677 South Segoe Road, Madison, WI 53711

Soil Science Society of America, 677 South Segoe Road, Madison, WI 53711

American Chemical Society, Education Division, 1155 16th Street, NW, Washington, DC 20036

National Environmental Health Association, 720 South Colorado Boulevard, Suite 970, Denver, CO 80222

Publications List:

George W. Ware: *Complete Guide to Pest Control*
Fundamentals of Pesticides: A Self-Instruction Guide
Drinking Water Health Advisories—Pesticides, U.S. EPA Office of Drinking Water and Office of Pesticides
100 Questions and Referenced Answers: Food Protection
Food Contamination from Environmental Sources, Nrigan/Simmons
Food Irradiation, World Health Organization
Botulism, Smith and Sugiyama
The Effects of Pesticides on Human Health, Baker/Wilkinson

Food and Service Sanitation Manual, Food and Drug Administration, 1976 ed, DHEH Pub. No. (FDA) 78-2081

P. Walton Purdom. *Environmental Health*, 2d ed. New York: Academic Press, 1980.

David F. Newton. *Elements of Environmental Health*. Columbus, Ohio: Charles E. Merrill Publishers, 1974

American Institute of Biological Sciences, 1401 Wilson Boulevard, Arlington, VA 22209

The National Pest Control Association, 250 West Jersey Street, Elizabeth, NJ 07207

The Humane Farming Association, 1550 California Street, Suite 6, San Francisco, CA 94109

Farm Animal Reform Movement, P.O. Box 30654, Bethesda, MD 20897-1425

American Farmland Trust, 1920 N Street, NW, Suite 400, Washington, DC 20036

Bioregional Project, HCR 3, Box 3, Brixey, MO 65618

Institute for Alternative Agriculture, 9200 Edmonston Road, Suite 117, Greenbelt, MD 20770

International Alliance for Sustainable Agriculture, Newman Center, University of Minnesota, 1701 University Avenue, SE, Room 202, Minneapolis, MN 55414

National Association of State Departments of Agriculture, 1616 H Street, NW, Washington, DC 20006

National Coalition to Stop Irradiation, P.O. Box 59-0488, San Francisco, CA 94159

National Farmers Union, Denver, CO 80251

National Future Farmers of America Organization, P.O. Box 15160, National FFA Center, Alexandria, VA 22309

Native Seeds/Search, 3950 West New York Drive, Tucson, AZ 85745

North American Farm Alliance, P.O. Box 2502, Ames, IA 50010

People, Food and Land Foundation, 35751 Oaks Springs Drive, Tollhouse, CA 93667

Woman's National Farm and Garden Association, 2402 Clearview Drive, Glenshaw, PA 15116

Alternative Farming Systems Information Center, National Agricultural Library, Room 111, Beltsville, MD 20705

Peter Singer. *Animal Liberation.* New York: Avon Books, 1975.

E Magazine, P.O. Box 6667, Syracuse, NY 13217

The American Minor Breeds Conservancy, P.O. Box 477, Pittsboro, NC 27312

Publications List:

"North American Livestock Census, 1985" (updated 1988)

"1987 Poultry Census and Sourcebook"

"The Chance to Survive"

"Preserving Our Livestock Heritage" (videotape)

John Robbins. *Diet for a New America.* Walpole, N.H.: Stillpoint Publishing, 1987.

Land Planners

When you think of the land, certain words may come to mind—vast, natural, inspiring, life giving, fertile, peaceful. The earth, the ground, the terrain, the soil, the beach, the sand, the grassland, the pasture, the meadow, the field, the desert, the property—all these terms evoke something infinite, permanent, necessary to life—good old terra firma. It's stable, it's supportive, it's basic, it's real.

We have been charged with its stewardship, with the responsibility of taking care of the land, of using it well, of passing it on in good condition to the next generation—fertile, verdant, wholesome. We should all be able to say that we "worship the ground we walk on."

Preserving the Earth

But are we able to say that honestly, or are there gaps in the care and feeding of the great Mother Earth? Many would answer "yes," and those people are probably actively employed in some way in providing for the proper use of the land. The land is simply not infinite; natural resources can be depleted if they are not carefully utilized and conserved. The soil can be contaminated, making it useless for growing or grazing. The vital ecological balance of plants and animals that are dependent on the earth for sustenance and, indeed, existence are in danger of extinction if their natural habitats are destroyed, thus putting all of life in jeopardy. For just as biologists, geologists, chemists and other environmental professionals must work together to ensure a healthy and wholesome life for all living things, all natural organisms are interdependent and must function as a team to survive.

Wildlife, farm animals, birds, plants, flowers, trees, and humans all depend on the earth for existence. But for too long we have abused the earth, thinking that it would always be there for our use. Or perhaps we weren't thinking at all. We became careless, we developed selfish interests in the use of the land, we forgot how important it is to us and future generations. There is no hidden or secret planet that can support life systems as we know them. So we have to take some serious steps to use the land that we still have appropriately, to consider all requests for its use, and work toward an equitable solution for its proper utilization.

Protective Laws and Government Agencies

We do have local and federal laws that will help us maintain public lands and some governmental agencies that are charged with protecting and preserving land-based natural resources. The Department of Interior's U.S. Geological Survey, the National Park Service, Bureau of Land Management, and Bureau of Reclamation all have responsibilities and, therefore, employment possibilities for people who are interested in land use and planning. The Forest Service of the Department of Agriculture, as well as municipal and state governments, employ land planners, landscape architects, surveyors, landscape designers, and plant scientists.

The National Park and Forest Services

The National Park and Forest services have been around since the beginning of the twentieth century, but increased awareness of the general environment occurred in the 1970s when laws were passed and agencies established to set and enforce standards. The National Environmental Policy Act provides for environmental impact statements for any project that will affect human life. The Endangered Species Act and the Federal Surface Mining and Reclamation Act of 1977 followed.

The Environmental Protection Agency

The Environmental Protection Agency (EPA) was established in 1970 by merging several other departments and agencies. The idea was to have a unified national program to solve environmental problems rather than relying on a wide variety of local ordinances throughout the country. The EPA is involved with these environmental concerns: air, water, pesticides, noise, drinking water, solid waste, toxic substances, and radiation. It is responsible for policy, standards, support, and evaluation of environmental factors through its regional offices. The EPA is also responsible for enforcing all laws concerning the environment.

The National Environmental Policy Act

In 1970, the National Environmental Policy Act (NEPA) became law. It was meant to establish a balance between human needs and the natural environment. Because of the NEPA, the Council on Environmental Quality was conceived to help the president determine sound environmental policy on a national basis. This council makes it necessary for all federal agencies to prepare environmental impact statements before they begin any major project, including construction of nuclear power plants, highways, and bridges.

A draft of all possibilities and ramifications is then given to federal, state, and local agencies for review and approval. After every responsible jurisdiction has commented on, objected to, revised, and resolved the problems, the EPA receives a copy, which then becomes available to the public.

These statements are extremely detailed and include probable and indirect ramifications on the ecology of a given area, short-term and long-term evaluations, and any possibilities of irretrievable damage to all aspects of the environment. And although the EPA cannot legally prevent another federal agency from going ahead with a project, it has the responsibility to advise the other agencies and the public of the environmental consequences.

These environmental impact statements can be crucial to land planners and architects. Further legislation that also affects these workers are the Coastal Zone Management Act, the Resource Conservation and Recovery Act of 1976, the Clean Air Act, and the Safe Drinking Water Act.

Land Planners

Land planners come in different professional guises and are true integrators and mediators between the technical necessities of a particular project and the aesthetic requirements for an attractive addition to the environment. Land planners may be found in cities, suburbs, rural areas, parks, and forests. They work in airports, for city governments, or with national transportation specialists. Whenever a new housing project, recreational area, shopping mall, or transportation system is being planned, the land planner will be involved.

What Land Planners Do

Planners have to know about local zoning regulations, pollution control laws, and building codes. They are responsible for taking in all points of view, such as the real estate developer, the historic preservation professional, the engineers and technicians, and the local citizenry, and come up with a plan that is environmentally harmonious and balanced. Besides the land, air and water safety must also be considered. In addition to all these factors, economic and social problems are part of the mix that the land planner has to deal with.

After initial discussions with the concerned parties, land planners study analyses of the soil, water, and air as well as any other natural resources that will be affected by the project. These may include plants, wildlife, insects, trees, and flowers.

The land planner also has to consider the goals of the project at this stage. For example, the goals of rehabilitating an urban neighborhood would be different from those of constructing an interstate highway. The land surrounding that which is actually being considered will also have to be investigated.

When all factors have been thoroughly studied, the land planner has to make proposals and recommendations for the wisest use of the land, based on function, environmental requirements, and cost. All this information is entered into a computer and analyzed with whatever technical data is needed until the final report is completed. Then these recommendations are made known to governmental agencies, other involved professionals, and the general public for review.

Educational Requirements

Land planners work with diverse populations using a wide variety of skills, including analysis, communication, diplomacy, and sometimes economics. If you decide to become a land planner, you have a couple of possible routes to take. You may prepare yourself during college, or you may combine education and work experience. At any rate, you should definitely plan an educational track that includes a master's degree.

If you are now in high school, you should begin to anticipate your undergraduate course work. Your major could be in planning, environmental studies, or urban studies. Your curriculum should include civil engineering, public administration, landscape architecture, natural science, and public health. Some social sciences, such as economics, political science or law, geography, and a strong base in both oral and written communications should round out your college studies. You should also try to develop strong decision-making and problem-solving skills as well as critical-thinking abilities. With this combination, you will be prepared to pursue your master's degree in planning.

If you have the opportunity during your summer breaks, it would be a good idea to get a job at the planning department in your hometown, to attend public hearings on land-use projects, to volunteer at your local zoning board, or to work on a neighborhood rehabilitation project.

If you already have your undergraduate degree and are working in a related field, you still need a master's degree, and it would also be a good idea to get some work experience in law, zoning, geography, resource economics, or urban planning.

Finding a Job

As you begin your job search, you may want to take a geographic approach; that is, find out where the jobs are and be willing to relocate in order to start your career. This approach might increase your chances of finding what you want. However, because of the need for land planners, you may very well be able to stay where you are and find a job with your local government, historic preservation group, or consulting group. If you work in a small town, you may be required to do everything—that is, take the project from beginning to end. In a larger city, you may be more specialized and departmentalized and work under the instruction and supervision of a more experienced planner.

The recognized professional organization for land planners is the American Planning Association. Members are entitled to a job listing service and publications on salary trends. Salaries, of course, will vary from state to state and agency to agency, but your entry-level salary with a master's degree should be about $24,000 a year.

Land planning seems to offer a rather bright future for people who are creative, analytical, proficient in communications skills, well versed in public policy and legislation, and dedicated to the goal of achieving environmental harmony and balance between humans, animals, and plants and the aesthetic and economic needs of the community.

Landscape Architects

Working closely with the land planner is the landscape architect. The American Society of Landscape Architecture states that there are about 25,000 landscape architects now working in the United States in both the public and private sectors, in universities, community services, and research.

Landscape architects play a vital role in the preservation of the environment by designing, planning, and managing the land. They are not only concerned with the beauty of the design but also with the environmental impact and best use of the land.

What Landscape Architects Do

Much like land planners, landscape architects work in urban, suburban, and rural settings, in parks, housing developments, national forests, or for a regional project encompassing a very large area. They must be able to solve problems, work with other professionals and community groups, speak and write English well, be proficient in graphic design, and have a deep commitment to the environment.

Landscape architects have to know about soil erosion, plant and animal relationships, and noise-absorbing vegetation. They usually work a great deal of the time on a site where a recreational facility, airport, highway, subdivision, industrial park, or shopping mall will be located. They may work for the municipal planning agency, a national park or forest, consulting firm, or developer. They work with planners, engineers, architects, and natural scientists, such as plant and animal physiologists.

In the process of their on-site analysis, they have to study the geography, topography, climate, and position of existing structures, such as buildings or bridges. Then they have to work on sketches, specifications, and budgetary requirements and eventually build an actual working model of the project. All details, such as roadways, parking facilities, walls, and fences must be included on this model.

Thus, their communication skills play a role because they have to prepare written reports, usually with detailed graphics, and make oral presentations on the feasibility of a particular project. Creativity, as well as highly developed technical skills, are needed at this stage of the process.

Educational Requirements

If you were the one in the family who liked to do the yard work, mow the lawn, plant the flower and vegetable gardens, trim the bushes, and prune the trees, you may be perfect for this line of work. But in addition to this basic aptitude, you will need a minimum of a college degree and, in some cases, a master's degree to become a landscape architect.

As an undergraduate, you will be taking natural and social sciences, behavioral sciences, art, mathematics, regional and environmental planning, and site analysis. Design, graphic arts, and communication skills will round out your program. A master's degree or doctorate is necessary if you want to be a university lecturer or engage in specialized research.

You will have to check to see if your state requires a license in addition to your degree in order to practice. This usually consists of passing an examination and may also include some supervised practice.

The accrediting agency for landscape architects is the Landscape Architectural Accreditation Board (LAAB). This agency sets the standards for all academic programs in the United States.

There are more than 45 accredited programs listed with the LAAB. When you decide that you want to follow through with a bachelor's program in landscape architecture, be sure to contact the LAAB. Then you will be on your way with a career that the Bureau of Labor Statistics names as one of the growth careers of the 1990s.

Types of Employment

If you work for the government on any level—city, county, state, or federal—you will be employed in national parks, recreation sites, and campgrounds. Municipal planning departments need architects for urban renewal and rehabilitation projects and land development and plaza design. You would also be utilized in waterfront developments, lighting design, selection of hazardous waste sites, and development of long-range policy and strategy.

Landscape architects who are in private practice design specific areas for commercial use, golf courses, zoos, pedestrian malls, transit systems, and recreational facilities. So the possibilities are good for a career as a landscape architect.

Salary Outlook

Entry-level landscape architects can expect a starting salary of about $20,000 annually, with those more experienced in the private sector earning from $25,000–$50,000 a year. The federal government, of course, goes on the GS pay schedule, so your pay would depend on your GS rating. You could probably fit into the $20,000–$40,000 range, depending on your education and experience.

Careers Related to Land Planning

As you can see, land planning, design, and management are only possible when various dedicated professionals share information;

analyze data; and make wise, safe, and healthy decisions based on ecological systems. For example, the land planner works with the realty specialist, who investigates all aspects of selling or leasing land, arranges for permits, and submits studies on the proper use of the land. Realty specialists may work with geologists, who have mapped the area that is being considered for use. The geologist uses maps that show minerals and bedrock in the area being considered for use and analyzes data collected from the actual site. They may all work with a cartographer, who designs maps of a specific area from aerial photos and other larger maps. All of these professionals are dependent on the work of the surveyor, who must be aware of the boundaries within which the project is to be constructed. With the help of surveyors, property disputes are avoided or ironed out based on titles and legal claims to the land.

Cartographers

The federal government needs people to fill all these job categories through the Bureau of Land Management or the U.S. Geological Survey, both units of the Department of the Interior.

The cartographer, for example, could get an entry-level position with the National Mapping Division, usually at the GS-5/7 level.

Charting maps of land areas is done either manually or digitally. At the GS-5 level, you would need a bachelor's degree or a combination of education (30 semester hours in cartography) and related work experience. If you want to qualify with your bachelor's degree alone, you have to have at least 30 semester hours of cartography, related physical science, computer science, or physical geography. In addition, you would have to have at least six semester hours of scientific math. If you choose to work for the government, you may find career opportunities at the Bureau of the Census, the Defense Mapping Agency, Federal Highway Administration, U.S. Army Corps of Engineers, U.S. Forest Service, or the Tennessee Valley Authority.

Geographers

Geographers, who are versed in both the natural and social sciences, are being called on more and more for their expertise in land-use problems. They study not only the location of natural phenomena but also the reason for that location. They analyze both physical and cultural aspects with emphasis on interpreting the ever-changing environment.

U.S. geographers have been involved in resource development such as the Tennessee Valley Authority and the Michigan Land Economic Survey in the 1930s. Later geographers became more and more involved with the social sciences and historical interpretation. Now they are employed by government and private agencies to research urban renewal, resource management, and highway systems. Sophisticated techniques used by contemporary geographers include remote sensing and statistical analyses to promote wise land use.

Those geographers who specialize in landforms and soil erosion may be called on to help in city planning or regional planning where geographic considerations are at stake. Geographers are uniquely qualified to study human relationships in regard to their physical environment.

Those of you who study geography can work as cartographers, land officers, and soil conservationists. Private businesses employ geographers to help them locate new industrial sites or plan transportation systems. City and county planners employ geographers in growing numbers because they often determine environmental considerations and risks.

Professional geographers should have a college degree in geography, with emphasis on statistical methods, computers, cartography, communication skills, foreign language, environmental studies, field techniques, meteorology, climatology, map design, and interpretation.

You should have at least 24 semester hours or 36 quarter hours past the introductory geography courses. If you desire a better paying job, you should consider obtaining a master's degree, which will include an internship plus 30–36 semester or 45–54 quarter hours. The entry-level salary range for the federal government is about $20,000–$26,000 annually. The federal government employs geographers at the Defense Mapping Agency, the National Oceanic and Atmospheric Administration, the Bureau of the Census, and the U.S. Geological Survey.

The professional organization for geographers is the Association of American Geographers. Membership includes annual meetings, journals, and a newsletter as well as special publications and job listings. A student membership is also available at reduced rates.

Working to Nurture the Land

These are some of the careers available to you if you want to work on planning, designing, preserving, and understanding the land and its relationship to human needs and nature's ecological demands. The land is vast, natural, inspiring, life giving, fertile, and peaceful. But we have to work to keep it that way. It is not infinite; it must be nurtured, cared for, and used, carefully and wisely, so that future generations will be able to enjoy its physical beauty and spiritual benefits. Natural beauty can be cultivated and enhanced. It can be saved from further destruction and can provide recreational space for millions.

Municipal planners know that our natural resources can be safe havens for the many residents who are so used to concrete, brick, glass, and steel as their everyday environment. Parks, gardens, and green spaces can be incorporated into all new and existing city plans for rejuvenation and rehabilitation of the urban environment. Even when new buildings must be built, the total natural environment must not be destroyed to accommodate them. Planners and architects must know how to coordinate human needs with the needs of other species that are also dependent on the land for survival.

Technicians are responsible for preserving and maintaining the land; geologists, geographers, surveyors, and cartographers are called on for resource development, often for larger regional projects that are frequently sponsored by the federal government. Understanding the land and its various functions, plotting it for possible use, understanding interrelationships, and interpreting pertinent data are some of their responsibilities. All work closely with land planners and landscape architects.

So if the land is your passion, you will have various opportunities to plan and preserve it with these careers. If you are creative and appreciate the many facets of human life and the diversity of other species, land planning and architecture may be where you'll fit into an environmental career.

You'll now have to decide which career path interests you most, how much time you want to devote to education and training, and maybe even how much physical work you may want to do. Some of these jobs involve working closely with others from different areas of expertise; some require supervisory skills. Others rely more on physical strength.

Many of these career opportunities are available through municipal, state, and federal governmental agencies. However, many private associations and organizations, although they may not have a large staff of employees, are good sources of information about specific areas of land preservation. You may wish to contact them to help you get started in your career search. They may also have volunteer programs on a limited basis.

Whichever career you choose, you will know that you are playing a vital role in the preservation of the beauties of the earth and all life forms dependent on it. And you will help to bring about a more beautiful environment for generations to come.

For Further Information

American Society of Landscape Architects, 4401 Connecticut Avenue, NW, Suite 500, Washington, DC 20008-2303

ASLA Publications:
  A Guide to Educational Programs in Landscape Architecture
  "Landscape Architecture Accredited Programs"
  "Between People and Nature"
American Planning Association, 1776 Massachusetts Avenue, NW, Washington, DC 20036
American Society of Consulting Planners, 210 Seventh Street, SE, Suite 647, Washington, DC 20003
Association of American Geographers, 1710 16th Street, NW, Washington, DC 20009
National Geographic Society, Geography Education Program, 17th and M Streets, NW, Washington, DC 20036
American Association of Botanical Gardens and Arboreta, P.O. Box 206, Swarthmore, PA 19081
Appalachian Regional Commission, 1666 Connecticut Avenue, NW, Washington, DC 20235
Archeological Conservancy, 415 Orchard Drive, Santa Fe, NM 87501
Canadian Arctic Resources Committee, 111 Sparks Street, Fourth Floor, Ottawa, Ontario K1P 5B5 Canada
Center for Plant Conservation, 125 Arborway, Jamaica Plain, MA 02130
Children of the Green Earth, P.O. Box 95219, Seattle, WA 98145
Grassland Heritage Foundation, 5460 Buena Vista, Shawnee Mission, KS 66205
Greensward Foundation, 104 Prospect Park, W, Brooklyn, NY 11215
International Erosion Control Association, P.O. Box 4904, Steamboat Springs, CO 80477
Landlab, Cal-Poly Pomona, 3801 West Temple Avenue, Pomona, CA 91768
Landscape Journal, The University of Wisconsin Press, 114 North Murray Street, Madison, WI 53715
Metropolitan Association of Urban Designers and Environmental Planners, P.O. Box 722, Church Street Station, New York, NY 10008
Missouri Prairie Foundation, P.O. Box 200, Columbus, MO 65205
Montana Land Reliance, P.O. Box 355, Helena, MT 59624
Montana Wilderness Association, P.O. Box 635, Helena, MT 59624
Outdoors Unlimited, P.O. Box 373, Kaysville, UT 84037
Save the Dunes Council, 444 Baker Road, Michigan City, IN 46360
Society for Ecological Restoration and Management, University of Wisconsin Arboretum, 1207 Seminole Highway, Madison, WI 53711
Tennessee Citizens for Wilderness Planning, 130 Tabor Road, Oak Ridge, TN 37830
Trust for Public Land, 116 New Montgomery Street, Fourth Floor, San Francisco, CA 94105
Trustees of Reservations, 572 Essex Street, Beverly, MA 01915
Urban Land Institute, 1090 Vermont Avenue, NW, Washington, DC 20005
Walden Forever Wild, P.O. Box 275, Concord, MA 01742

U.S. Geological Survey, Personnel Office, 345 Middlefield Road, MS-213, Menlo Park, CA 94025

Personnel Officer, Bureau of the Census, Room 3260, Washington, DC 20233

Defense Mapping Agency, Attn: PRSD, Washington, DC 20315-0300

Department of the Interior, Bureau of Land Management, Chief, Division of Cadastral Survey, 18th and C Streets, NW, Washington, DC 20240

National Oceanic and Atmospheric Administration, Washington Science Center, Building 5, 6010 Executive Building, Rockville, MD 20852

U.S. Forest Service, Personnel Officer, P.O. Box 96090, Washington, DC 20090

National Park Service, Main Interior Building, Room 2328, P.O. Box 37127, Washington, DC 20013-7127

Environmental Protection Agency Headquarters, Personnel Services, Room 3020, 401 M Street, SW, Washington, DC 20460

CHAPTER FIVE

Foresters, Conservation Scientists, and Resource Managers

L and planners and landscape architects, geographers and geologists, agronomists and plant physiologists, botanists and ecologists—all tend to the needs of the earth and the demands of human life, from a certain perspective. We'll see, as we explore the various career opportunities for nature lovers, that other professionals take care of the land, water, air, plants, and animals in a number of different ways.

We might also note here that the conservation and preservation of natural resources is a multidimensional and integrated search for solutions to the many problems of stewardship. So a biologist may work in a zoo or a forest; a geologist may study oceans, space, or earthquakes. A botanist could be employed on a farm, in a university setting, or in a park.

A full complement of environmental professionals could at any time be working in a city park or national forest, a rural development or suburban industrial site—all concerned with some aspect of environmental safety and human need. And each environmentally oriented citizen can offer valuable insights regarding the design or purpose of an area under consideration for use.

Forests: A Valuable Resource

The forests of our nation and the world are always in need of special care because they have one of the most important natural resources—trees. As well as trees, there is a wide variety of other life forms dependent on the natural ecological balance of the forest. Coexisting in the forest are grass, soil, rocks, air, water, wildlife, plants, and minerals; all participate in complex interrelationships. The National Forest Service manages 191 million acres of forest land, and there are more than 700 million acres of forest land outside that system, so many people with diverse skills are needed to make sure that our forests are well maintained.

Different types of forests include municipal, county, community, and federal parks; rangelands and wildlife sanctuaries; swampland; watersheds; and timberland and wilderness areas. Some of these areas are used for recreation; others, for habitat restoration. Some are used for logging; others, for wildlife protection. Some are used for cattle grazing; others, for animal rehabilitation.

There seems to be a growing awareness of the interrelatedness or holism of the forests and the life forms they conserve and protect. Those who work in forests and parks are truly resource managers, because these lands must be protected from exploitation and unscrupulous development.

Preserving Forests

Both independent and government organizations and agencies are working, sometimes together, sometimes at odds with each other, to effectively manage, preserve, and restore the land and its resources. Private, state, and national forests may serve several purposes—recreational, industrial, and environmental—and sometimes these purposes do not coincide. For example, the paper industry needs wood from the trees in the forest, but trees remove carbon dioxide from the air and reduce the chance of global warming. Trees are also natural habitats for various species of wildlife and birds, such as the spotted owl. So conflicts arise between the human need for employment and paper, which the logging industry provides, and the growing awareness among private citizen groups of the importance of preserving the precious balance of nature.

Human recreational activities in parks and forests may also have harmful effects on the diverse life forms there. This may also cause friction between sportspeople, athletes, and campers, who wish to use the facilities and natural resources of the forest, and the independent environmental groups that carefully monitor habitat destruction, endangerment of species, and waste of resources.

When governmental agencies that are charged with stewardship of public lands engage in practices that will adversely affect the life of various species in parks or forests, environmentally oriented organizations protest the action. When land developers or oil companies threaten to destroy animal or plant habitats, they can also expect vociferous protest from these same organizations.

Much research is being done regarding the necessity of tropical rain forests in the preservation of vital ecosystems affecting global resources. Still more research has to be done on forests and trees to see what effect they have on the total environment. However, many companies and industries are beginning to use recycled paper products so that fewer trees will have to be cut and less garbage will be produced and disposed of.

Careers in Forest Conservation

Passions run high when it comes to natural resource management and preservation, especially considering how many millions of acres are involved. And when you choose a career in conservation of parks or forests, you should think about whether you want to work for a governmental agency that has to follow the policy of the current administration or for an independent, grass-roots organization that targets a specific species or devotes itself to playing the watchdog role for a variety of environmental issues. Whichever path you choose, commitment, education, endurance, skill, creativity, training, knowledge of the law, and, sometimes, physical strength will determine your career path.

Federal Government Jobs in Forestry

Let's start our exploration with the federal government. The National Forest Service is part of the Department of the Interior and currently employs 33,000 permanent employees and another 12,000–15,000 temporary employees. The service has three branches: the national forest system, state and private forestry, and research. As part of the national forest system, the resources that have to be tended are the soil, water, air, wildlife, trees, and land, which comprise almost two-thirds of all federally owned land.

If you work with the state and private forestry branch, you will share information in fire prevention, insect and disease control, forest planning, and land development. You may also help with marketing products that are forest related. This cooperative work may be technical or financial and may extend beyond the borders of the United States.

The Forest Service employs researchers who develop programs that help solve ecological problems throughout this country, such as tree growth and harvesting, rangeland management, animal and fish habitats, recreation, and monitoring. This branch cooperates with other federal agencies in the United States and with foreign countries through private agreement.

We're going to look at some of the careers that are listed in the technical category. Included in the technical category are biologists, foresters, and engineers and their technicians. In each of these fields, people who operate and repair equipment and maintain machines are needed. And many of the same careers that we have already looked at, such as biologist, botanist, landscape architect, land planner, soil scientist, and plant physiologist, may turn up here or in the parks of this country. We'll also take a look at how they, along with ornithologists and animal rehabilitators, might function in a forest or park.

Foresters
What Foresters Do

At the heart of the forest is the forester, who manages the complexities of the forest. He or she is a highly skilled and trained professional who knows about the relationships of all life forms in the forest and how to cope with the changes that occur when, for instance, a certain type of tree ceases to exist and another type grows in its place.

Foresters also have to supervise all recreational activities in the forest, such as skiing, hiking, swimming, and camping. Performing that responsibility may include planning needed surveys, recommending land acquisition, writing reports and recommendations, and occasionally speaking to the public about conservation policies regarding the forest.

The type of animals in a forest will determine what foresters must do for their protection and health. For example, foresters have to know how many of certain types of animals a forest can accommodate and what kind of shrubs and grasses they may need for sustenance. Wildlife, domestic animals, and sheep all have different needs that foresters are responsible to meet.

If lumber is a major product of the forest, foresters have to know the size of the trees and how much lumber they can yield. When foresters decide which trees are to be cut, they also have to decide which trees will replace them. If there is a forest fire, it may be necessary to replace a large section of the forest. As a forester, you may also be able to choose a specialty, such as research, fire prevention, disease control, soil erosion, or logging practices. In addition to very specific knowledge about forest ecology, foresters have to supervise and train other workers, know all the laws and enforce them, travel when necessary, and react quickly to emergencies.

Qualifications

You will need a bachelor's degree in forestry and some practical experience to become a forester. Field trips and camps sponsored by forestry schools will also give you a feel for this type of work. Or you can use your summer breaks to work in a city or state park or forest or volunteer at a grass-roots environmental group. Some colleges may accept this work as part of your credits. The U.S. Forest Service has a volunteer program, and you can get an application form by writing to the U.S. Forest Service, Department of Agriculture, Human Resource Programs, P.O. Box 2417, Washington, DC 20013.

In addition to your forestry courses, you will have to have highly developed oral and written communication skills, mathematics, biometrics, and computer knowledge. If you choose to specialize in a particular field or to engage in research, you will have to have an advanced degree. Specialties include wildlife conservation, entomology, genetics, tree culture, wood technology, or recreation.

Where to Find Jobs

Other federal agencies employing foresters are the Bureau of Land Management, the National Park Service, the Bureau of

Indian Affairs, and the Tennessee Valley Authority. Every state has some agency concerned with forests, parks, and conservation that will provide career opportunities for foresters. Urban forestry, which involves tree planting in city parks and streets, is a new field with growing possibilities, and private consulting firms as well as grass-roots environmental groups hire foresters.

So, as you can see, opportunities for foresters exist in national, state, and private forests and in cities, industry, and independent organizations. You may choose to become a forest technician or work in a nursery for a while before committing to the additional educational requirements of foresters.

Forest Technicians
What Forest Technicians Do

The forest technician's work in forests and parks is of vital necessity to the proper use of the land. Much of your work will have to do with patrolling the land, preserving it from ravaging fires, and protecting trees and various life forms that are dependent on them.

As a forest technician, you would be called on to assist foresters in planting trees, preventing fires, and constructing roads. One type of technician is the surveyor, who maps out where roads will be built. Other technicians are responsible for the health of the trees, so they inspect for harmful insects and diseases; prune or destroy trees when necessary; and pollinate, graft, and gather seeds under the supervision of the forester or plant scientist.

You may need supervisory skills if you oversee work crews for road building and repair, planting trees, and fighting fires. Some map interpretation and data collecting as well as report writing may be part of your job. Many tools are required to keep parks and forests in good condition, and you may have to use and repair them. You may also have to maintain buildings, do carpentry work, and purchase provisions for work crews.

Your work will change with the seasons throughout the country. Planting will be carried out at certain times; harvesting, at others. Most of your work will be outdoors, and you may also have to live in the park or forest where you work. You will also have to be ready to handle emergencies in any area of the park, no matter what the weather conditions are. Because you often have to travel long distances in a large park or forest, you should have physical stamina. You will often have to walk on rugged terrain while carrying heavy supplies. Or you may have to ride a horse or travel in a helicopter to cover all the territory in your jurisdiction.

Qualifications

You will need a high school diploma to become a forest technician. Your diploma may be from a vocational high school, but your studies should include math and science. Since you may have to communicate with the public and write reports, you should have solid communication skills, too.

After high school, you should have at least two years experience in forestry. This can be accomplished on the job or in school. Valuable work experience includes farming, logging, surveying, or construction. You will also probably have to have a driver's license because you will have to drive trucks and maybe even farm equipment, such as tractors.

During your summer vacations, you may want to work in a local park or forest, state conservation bureau, or with the U.S. Forest Service. The Bureau of Land Management may also have summer jobs available. The National Park Service offers a Volunteers in the Parks (VIP) program for those who wish to try their hand at this work before committing to an actual career. You can apply through any one of the regional offices.

Technicians in parks and forests may have a choice, at this time, of seasonal or temporary work. There will also be more work in the more heavily forested parts of the country. As the economy improves and more people become involved in the recreational and environmental uses of the forest, forest technician jobs may increase.

With your high school diploma and two years of additional schooling, on-the-job experience may put you in line for more responsibilities. But you will need more education if you want to become a forester or park ranger.

At this time it is somewhat difficult to predict the career prospects for foresters and technicians because of the economy and demand for paper products. With more and more individuals and corporations recycling paper products, the demand for paper may decrease. There may be an increased demand for recreational facilities in the future, but you may have to be willing to relocate to more heavily forested areas or work for city parks and forests, land developers, or nurseries. You will probably make more money working for private industry than for government, but entry-level salaries will vary with your experience and training.

Federal Government Jobs in Parks

The Department of the Interior administers the National Park Service, which is charged with the responsibility of managing and protecting 77 million acres of natural, cultural, historic, and recreational areas across the country. In addition to 49 national parks, the service administers preserves, seashores, rivers, parkways, and recreation areas. Because of this, the Park Service offers a wide variety of career choices. It currently has 7,500 permanent jobs, and, during the summer, this number could reach more than 21,000. This figure includes permanent, full-time, temporary, and part-time positions. As with all federal government jobs, they are filled through the Office of Personnel Management.

Most national parks are not located near cities, so you may have to relocate to find a job and eventually be transferred if you want to further your career. The Park Service is looking for well-qualified personnel, but competition for jobs is high.

Park Rangers

What Park Rangers Do

At the heart of the park system are the park rangers, whose primary responsibilities include management of wildlife, lakeshores, seashores, and recreation areas. When you first start out, you may be assigned to operate campsites by supplying firewood, assigning sites, and providing security. You may be employed in a city or rural park, and most of your work will be done outdoors.

Much of your work has to do with patrolling the park to prevent unlawful hunting, enforce regulations, inspect trees for disease, and report dangerous situations and emergencies to the park supervisor. Some of your work will also be educating the public on natural and historical features, giving informational speeches, and assisting with research projects.

Park rangers have to instruct the public on safety procedures for water sports, prevention of fires and accidents, and administering first aid. So you'll have to develop good communication skills for educational purposes and also because you may have to settle disputes or clear up misunderstandings among park users.

Qualifications

Park rangers need a high school diploma, a driver's license, and one year's park-related experience. This could include recreation work, tourism, or resource management.

If you don't have this experience, college courses in natural science, park and recreation management, or police science could substitute. You would then receive six months of training with the service and the possibility for promotion would be to district ranger, park manager, or staff specialist. Further education may also be required for these promotions. Jobs with the service are competitive, but the future is looking better because of increased interest in the environment and because of recreational possibilities in the national parks.

Salary Prospects

You'll probably begin your career as a ranger at the GS-2, GS-3, or GS-4 level. The annual salary range is $12,385–$19,725. You may earn slightly more in the private sector. The U.S. Forest Service, the National Park Service, and the U.S. Fish and Wildlife Service also employ biologists, botanists, soil scientists, plant physiologists, geologists, zoologists, and ornithologists.

Ornithologists

What Ornithologists Do

Ornithologists study birds, including their ecology, physiology, anatomy, and behavior. In order to be competitive for jobs, you will have to have at least a bachelor's degree, and in many cases a master's degree is preferred.

There are more than 200 professionals working in ornithological jobs in North America today, and competition for jobs is tight. If you want to work outdoors, you'll probably want to work for a governmental agency rather than in a university or museum.

Any experience with birds will be helpful because much of your job as an ornithologist has to do with observing and marking birds. If you are an avid bird watcher, you may have the beginnings of an ornithological career. With that as an avocation, you may want to work as a volunteer or seasonal employee at a park, forest, refuge, zoo, or field station. The more exposure you have to fieldwork or research, the better prepared you will be for your career.

Qualifications

You will have to have a bachelor's degree to be an ornithologist. Your undergraduate courses should include biology, botany, zoology, math, biochemistry, and statistics. Tackle as many research projects as possible in college and study computer science and foreign languages as well as English.

Where Ornithologists Work

With governmental agencies, you will be involved in the general field of wildlife management, which includes preservation and study of individual birds and also various species. The U.S. Fish and Wildlife Service administers more than 400 wildlife refuges, all employing ornithologists. The service also administers research facilities throughout the country. Most national parks also employ ornithologists. You should also check out your state, county, and municipal parks and forest systems. At the federal level, you would probably enter at GS-5 with an annual salary range of $16,973–$22,067.

State conservation agencies need ornithologists, either as part of general wildlife projects or as part of specialized projects concerned with birds only. Field ornithologists are needed for state projects involving endangered and threatened species or status surveys. Independent organizations focusing on the preservation of bird species are the National Wildlife Federation and Ducks Unlimited. The Nature Conservancy and the National Audubon Society manage sanctuaries where you might find your career opportunity. Nature centers also employ ornithologists.

So if birds are your passion, there are opportunities for you if you have the inclination and the education. The professional organization you might want to contact for further information is The American Ornithologists' Union in Washington, D.C.

Range Managers
What Range Managers Do

Managing grazing land for both livestock and wildlife also offers opportunities for employment for nature lovers who want to work outdoors. This land is often called the range, and it also needs managers or conservationists. Often these lands are used for recreation and as natural habitats for animals. As a range manager, you would decide which animals would graze on them and select the proper grazing seasons.

Sometimes you would work as a combination forester, wildlife conservationist, soil erosion specialist, and habitat rehabilitator. You will need to know about vegetation, watershed processes, farming, and ecological interrelationships.

Qualifications

To become a range manager, you need a bachelor's degree in that field. You course work might include biology, chemistry, physics, plant and animal physiology, and soil sciences. Your knowledge of English and computers as well as wildlife and forestry is helpful.

Because most of the nation's rangeland is in the West, you may have to relocate to find employment as a range manager. Federal jobs are available through the Forest Service and Bureau of Land Management. State conservation agencies may also provide career opportunities. You can also find employment on privately owned ranches or at universities doing research.

Salary Outlook

You would probably start out at the GS-5, GS-6, or GS-7 level with the federal government, with an entry-level starting salary range of $16,973–$27,332 per year. Salaries will vary from state to state and ranch to ranch.

Since more and more people are concerned with the environment, there is a growing need for people who can restore, rehabilitate, and improve the rangelands. So your future looks bright as a range manager if you have a little cowboy or cowgirl in you.

Land Developers versus Environmentalists

Protecting the wildlife, fish, birds, and trees on the nation's many acres of public land requires a wide variety of professionals with a deep commitment to all species affected by man-made change. Natural disasters, such as floods and fires, are traumatic enough to all life forms. But when humans carelessly take other creatures' home and food and even separate them from their young, it is a tragic destruction of their natural habitat. All that is left are inhabitable buildings and concrete roads.

One of the struggles over public lands today is going on between land developers and environmentalists. Developers make their living by building new structures that supposedly fill some human need, whether it is recreational or commercial. Many people believe, along with many developers, that human needs supersede the needs of all other species and that housing and food for humans are more important than for other life forms. Environmentalists are generally not in complete accord with this belief, and that is where problems arise.

The approach to solving such problems is becoming more and more holistic or integrated, with many committed professionals trying to preserve all species in healthy and nurturing habitats. When we lose any species, we know that we will never be able to retrieve it—it is gone forever. And that has already happened to many species. Others are hanging on to existence, often in a totally unnatural environment. Many range managers, wildlife managers, biologists, foresters, and park rangers work in their own areas to try to reclaim certain habitats or to prevent further destruction through development. Land planners and landscape architects are also called in to investigate the ecology of an area before developers can build a building, a road, a shopping mall, or recreational facility.

More and more regulations are tending to require developers who destroy a wildlife habitat to construct another comparable one. In the case of fish, a new fishery would have to be constructed. These species need not even be threatened or endangered for this to happen.

For this reason, some developers and corporations may hire specialists to restore habitats. These might include wildlife biologists, fish biologists, and culturists. State governments are also becoming aware of habitat problems as new suburban housing developments encroach on homes of deer, beaver, gophers, and raccoons who forage for food in garbage cans because their natural food supply has been destroyed. Or they may move into the garage, basement, or attic, seeking shelter because the trees and bushes that have protected them are gone.

Instead of destroying the wildlife and their habitat, more and more ecologically minded professionals are trying to make sure that new habitats are built or remnants of the old ones are restored. Refuges and sanctuaries also often serve as shelters for displaced animals. And fish farms are becoming more popular, partially because we have polluted our waters so badly that fish are no longer able to spawn in our rivers, oceans, lakes, and streams.

Animal Rehabilitators
What Animal Rehabilitators Do

Sometimes, in the midst of all the natural destruction, whether due to oil spills, land development, highway construction, forest fires, floods, trapping, hunting, or poaching, actual animals are injured and harmed, shot or maimed. Birds can't fly, fish can't swim. When this happens to wildlife, the animal rehabilitator has to be called in.

Generally speaking, these are usually wildlife and fishery biologists who work at either private or public rehabilitation centers. As a rehabilitator, you would have course work in anatomy and physiology, shock cycles, drugs and medications, and physical therapy. Wounds have to be treated and broken bones mended. Birds, fish, and animals in oil spills have to be thoroughly cleaned before caring for any other medical problem they may have sustained.

It would be a good idea for you to volunteer at an animal shelter, veterinarian hospital, or state park and work with animals who are under stress, in shock, or injured before you commit yourself to this career. It is difficult to deal with injured animals but very necessary in order to preserve and conserve the natural environment. Animal rehabilitators are on the front line of protection and preservation of wildlife, birds, and fish. With the threat of further water, air, and land pollution, the rehabilitator will be in greater demand.

As we have seen, many highly skilled professionals and technicians are needed just to meet today's environmental needs of our forests and parks, wildlife, trees, birds, and fish. Common, as well as endangered, species of animals and plants must be protected as well as livestock, grasslands, and wetlands.

How you want to contribute to the local, state, or federal parks and forest or to private industry or grass-roots organizations may depend on how much time you want to devote to education and training and whether you want to specialize in forestry or wildlife biology, ornithology or fish. If you're more comfortable on the ranch or farm, you may want to become a range manager. The future holds many potential changes as land, water, and air continue to be threatened with pollution, development, and technology. Increasing regulations and awarenesswillnecessitate a world full of committed professionals seeking to solve complex environmental problems. You may be one of the lucky ones to participate in the process.

For Further Information

American Conservation Association, 30 Rockefeller Plaza, Room 5402, New York, New York 10112

American Forest Council, 1250 Connecticut Avenue, NW, Suite 320, Washington, DC 20036

American Forestry Association, 1516 P Street, NW, Washington, DC 20005

American Recreation Coalition, 1331 Pennsylvania Avenue, NW, #726, Washington, DC 20004

American Trails, 1400 16th Street, NW, Washington, DC 20036

Canadian Parks and Wilderness Society, 69 Sherbourne Street, Suite 313, Toronto, Ontario M5A 3X7 Canada

Forest Farmers Association, 4 Executive Park East, P.O. Box 95385, Atlanta, GA 30347

Forestry Canada/Fôrets Canada, Place Vincent Massey, 351 St. Joseph Boulevard, Hull, Quebec K1A 1G5 Canada

Friends of the Boundary Waters Wilderness, 1313 5th Street, SE, Suite 329, Minneapolis, MN 55414

Grasslands Heritage Foundation, 5460 Buena Vista, Shawnee Mission, KS 66205

International Society for the Preservation of the Tropical Rainforest, 3931 Camino de la Cumbre, Sherman Oaks, CA 91423

International Society of Arboriculture, P.O. Box 908, 303 West University Avenue, Urbana, IL 61801

International Society of Tropical Foresters, 5400 Grosvenor Lane, Bethesda, MD 20814

Land Trust Exchange, 1017 Duke Street, Alexandria, VA 22314

National Arbor Day Foundation, 100 Arbor Avenue, Nebraska City, NE 68410

National Association of State Foresters, c/o Forest, Park, and Wildlife Services, 580 Taylor Avenue, Annapolis, MD, 21501-2351

National Association of State Recreation Planners, 205 Butler Street, NE, Suite 1352, Atlanta, GA 30334

National Audubon Society, 950 Third Avenue, New York, NY 10022

National Council of the Paper Industry for Air and Stream Improvement, 260 Madison Avenue, New York, NY 10016

National Inholders Association, 30 West Thomson, Box 588, Sonoma, CA 95476

National Parks and Conservation Association, 1015 31st Street, NW, Washington, DC 20007

National Recreation and Park Association, 3101 Park Center Drive, Alexandria, VA 22302

National Wildflower Research Center, 2600 FM 973 North, Austin, TX 78725

North American Family Campers Association, P.O. Box 328, Concord, VT 05824

Rainforest Action Network, 301 Broadway, Suite A, San Francisco, CA 94133

Rainforest Alliance, 270 Lafayette Street, Suite 512, New York, NY 10012

Save-the-Redwoods League, 114 Sansone Street, Room 605, San Francisco, CA 94104

Society for Range Management, 1839 York Street, Denver, CO 80206

Society for American Foresters, 5400 Grosvenor Lane, Bethesda, MD 20014

TreePeople, 12601 Mulholland Drive, Beverly Hills, CA 90210

Trees for Life, 1103 Jefferson, Wichita, KS 67203

Trees for Tomorrow, 611 Sheridan Street, P.O. Box 609, Eagle River, WI 54521

Western Forestry and Conservation Association, 4033 SW Canyon Road, Portland, OR 97221

Wilderness Society, 1400 I Street, NW, Suite 550, Washington, DC 20005

American Association of Wildlife Veterinarians, Department of Veterinary Pathology, Iowa State University, Ames, IA 50011

American Fisheries Society, 5410 Grosvenor Lane, Bethesda, MD 20814

American Ornithologists' Union, National Museum of Natural History, Smithsonian Institution, Washington, DC 20560

Canadian Society of Environmental Biologists, P.O. Box 962, Station F, Toronto, Ontario M4Y 2N9 Canada

Cooper Ornithological Society, Department of Biology, University of California, Los Angeles, CA 90024-1606

Endangered Species Act Reauthorization Coordinating Committee, 1725 De Sales Street, NW, Suite 500, Washington, DC 20036

Friends of Animals and Their Environment, P.O. Box 7283, Minneapolis, MN 55407

Funds for Animals, 200 West 57th Street, New York, NY 10019

Humane Society of the U.S., 2100 L Street, NW, Washington, DC 20037

International Wildlife Rehabilitation Council, 1171 Kellogg Street, Suisun, CA 94585

National Institute for Urban Wildlife, 10921 Trotting Ridge Way, Columbia, MD 21044-2831

National Wildlife Rehabilitators Association, R.R. 1, Box 125E, Brighton, IL 62012

Organization of Wildlife Planning, Box 7921, Madison, WI 53707

Western Bird Banding Association, 3975 North Pontatoc, Tucson, AZ 85718

Wetlands for Wildlife, P.O. Box 344, West Bend, WI 53095

Wildlife Management Institute, 1101 14th Street, NW, Suite 725, Washington, DC 20005

Wildlife Society, 5410 Grosvenor Lane, Bethesda, MD 20814

Long Point Bird Observatory, P.O. Box 160, Port Rowan, Ontario N0E 1M0 Canada

Point Reyes Bird Observatory, 4990 Shoreline Highway, Stinson Beach, CA 94970

Manomet Bird Observatory, Box O, Manomet, MA 02345

"Employment Opportunities in the U.S. Fish and Wildlife Service," Department of the Interior, Washington, DC 20240

"Careers in the United States Department of the Interior," Superintendent of Documents, U.S. Government Printing Office, Washington, DC 20402

Careers in Geology

Geologists

*I*f people have told you that you have "rocks in your head," maybe you're cut out to be a geologist! Rocks are exactly what geologists have on their minds, especially in their relationship to the earth's changes. These natural changes occur through volcanic eruptions, earthquakes, and erosion. So here we are, back to the earth. Agronomists, biologists, geographers, land planners, soil scientists, range managers, foresters—all are concerned with preservation of the land.

What Geologists Do

Geologists approach the earth from another angle. They study the earth's composition, evolution, its past, and future. They do this by investigating rocks and fossils, continental shifts, and natural resources. Fieldwork is important to geologists because they have to collect samples and survey and map land areas. They collect rocks and fossils as well as minerals and classify and analyze them. Some of this analysis may take place in the laboratory.

As a result of all this, they know where rocks and minerals are located, how thick formations are, and in which direction they are formed. Geologists are also concerned with water, gas, oil, and coal. They study the earth's surface and substrata and often do their work in the ocean.

Geologists' work is important to land planners because geologists can determine whether a specific area is strong enough to support buildings, highways, or bridges. Their work with seismologists helps to predict earthquakes and volcanoes. Their work in the ocean helps us understand its mineral content and heat flow. Geologists work with environmentalists to clean up waste material in the water and on land. As a geologist, then, you may work in isolated camps, in deserts, forests, or oceans throughout the world. You may work for private industry, governmental agencies, or nonprofit organizations.

Where Geologists Work

Engineering, gas production, and petroleum companies employ geologists who find most of their work in the United States in the South, the West, and Alaska. You could also work for state, county, or federal governments. The federal agencies that employ geologists are the U.S. Geological Survey, the U.S. Department of the Interior, the Bureau of Reclamation, the Bureau of Mines, the Department of Energy, the Forest Service, the Environmental Protection Agency, and the Nuclear Regulatory Commission. With some experience, you may even be able to work as a private consultant.

Important Characteristics and Qualifications

You will have to be physically strong and like to work under all kinds of climatic conditions if you are going to be a geologist. Geologists in the field usually work together in groups or in teams and have to be able to get along with other people.

If you're still in high school and have those "rocks in your head," you should study English and foreign languages and have a firm footing in math and science. You will eventually have to have a bachelor's degree and maybe even a master's degree. Industrial employers are increasingly looking for the master's degree; university professors and researchers should have a Ph. D. Suggested courses in college should include chemistry, physics, biology, engineering, and math in addition to geology. Further study may include hydrology, geophysics, petrology, marine geology, or even paleontology. Many colleges and universities here and in Canada offer degrees in geology, but you should check the requirements and curricula before you select a college or university for undergraduate work.

Salary Outlook

Once you have acquired your education, you will probably find out that the highest salaries are found in the private sector; government generally has a lower pay scale. Salaries vary, of course, but you can probably count on starting at about $25,000 a year with a bachelor's degree and approximately $35,000 with an advanced degree.

Learning about Geology Careers

You may want to work with a state or county agency as a volunteer or part-time worker in order to see if geology is for you. Since geologists work with other scientists and professionals, you could work in a local park or forest with surveyors or cartographers, urban land planners, or engineers during your summer breaks or vacations. You might also work for a local waste management firm, seismologist, oceanographer, or mineralogist.

This part-time or volunteer work can also give you a better idea about job opportunities in the various areas of specialization in the agency or industry you choose. As the economy improves, jobs will, of course, open up. However, many government and industrial organizations have streamlined their operations, and this streamlining may remain in effect in the future. Your education and training will be your best bet in finding a job because the field is becoming more and more technically demanding. Computer and communication skills, laboratory work, and research will also be advantageous in seeking employment.

Professional organizations are also helpful for finding your niche in the work world. Primary among them are the American Geological Institute, the American Association of Petroleum Geologists, and the Geological Society of America. These organizations can provide you with additional information in your search for the rocks and fossils that will make up the rest of your life study as a geologist.

As a nature-loving geologist, much of your effort in the future will be directed toward improvement of our natural resources, including cleaning up any pollution of our water supply. Together with hydrologists and engineers, you will be called upon to contribute to the clean-up process.

Hydrologists

The environment demands committed work from a variety of professionals, and hydrologists play an integral part in the continuing efforts to maintain the quality of our water. Hydrologists study the location of water on the earth and how it behaves. This study is crucial to our knowledge and understanding of our water supply, how it is used, how much we have, and what forms it takes.

What Hydrologists Do

Hydrologists measure bodies of water and check the amount of underground water, too. Since some of our water comes from snow and rain, hydrologists' work is similar to that of meteorologists. Hydrologists study water as it exists as a liquid, solid, or gas and, therefore, they necessarily work with glaciers, ice, and snow. Since so much water runs through rocks, hydrologists often work with geologists.

Hydrologists collect water samples and analyze them for quantity and quality. They can recommend, based on these results, the most efficient use of the resources we have and predict future needs. It is estimated that our country alone spends $10 million annually on water resource development.

Included in water resource development is water conservation, water quality planning, and the protection of watersheds, Studying water pollution, predicting floods, solving water shortage problems, and forecasting drought are also included. So the hydrologist's work will affect everyone's lives and contributes a great deal to the preservation of the environment.

Hydrologists' data also assist in solving water power, irrigation, crop production, and navigation problems. They may also assist in planning farm ponds, sewers, drainage systems, and dams. Erosion, sedimentary deposits, snowfall—all are part of the total picture that the hydrologist must investigate and analyze.

If you become an oceanographic hydrologist, you may assist fishing, shipping, and mining enterprises. You may also be involved in international cooperative ventures since all countries are bound by common oceans, rivers, and lakes and their effects on our lives.

Qualifications and Educational Requirements

Much of your work will be outdoors with some light to moderate physical work. Good eyesight, creativity, and the ability to share information and work well with others are valuable characteristics for hydrologists. Report writing will also be a part of your job, and, in many cases, knowledge of computers will be necessary.

Hydrologists need to know, among other sciences, chemistry, physics, biology, geology, geophysics, geomorphology, soil science, and math. Environmental and mining engineering, ecology, and meteorology are also major components of the mix of disciplines necessary to solve the problems of water resources.

For either the private or public sector, you must have a bachelor's degree with 30 semester hours of course work, including any combination of hydrology, physical sciences, engineering science, soils, math, aquatic biology, and the management or conservation of water resources. Math courses have to include differential and integral calculus and physics. The U.S. Geological Survey also recommends atmospheric science, meteorology, geology, oceanography, and atmospheric science. It may also accept an appropriate combination of education and experience.

Where to Find Jobs

Hydrology is said to be one of the "hot" new career tracks, with many opportunities both in the private and public sectors. A master's degree is in great demand in private industry, which includes consulting and chemical engineering firms and waste disposal firms.

Hydrologists work in forestry, range management, public health, and energy development. They can be found in the mountains or deserts, on farms or in cities. Interrelationships with rocks, dynamics of bodies of water, surface and groundwater, moisture in the soil, sediment, and precipitation all fall in the boundaries of the hydrologists' work.

Government Careers

State and local governments also hire hydrologists, with the primary federal employer being the U.S. Geological Survey. The U.S. Forest Service, Department of Energy, National Oceanic and Atmospheric Administration, the Bureau of Reclamation, and the U.S. Army Corps of Engineers are also employers of hydrologists. It has been estimated that 9,000 people are now employed in water resources in the United States.

If you work for the government, you should have completed course work in engineering, surveying, drafting, physical science, biology, or math to qualify at the GS-3 federal level. If you want to enter at the GS-4 level, you'll need two years of study including at least 12 semester hours; and for the GS-5 entry-level requirement, you'll need four years of course work leading to the bachelor's degree in science, engineering, construction, or industrial technology. Beyond that level, you will need two years of graduate work or a master's degree.

The Water Resources Division of the U.S. Geological Survey employs almost 5,000 people in the United States, Puerto Rico, Guam, and the Virgin Islands. Its mission is to manage the nation's water supply to the optimum using hydrologic information gathered by hydrologists and hydrologic technicians. The annual budget is close to $180 million.

This division works with state and local government agencies as well as other federal agencies and governments in Southeast Asia, Africa, Saudi Arabia, and China. This may give you and idea of how extensive, comprehensive, and important the study of conservation of water is on a global basis.

The Geological Survey offers other programs that may be of interest to you as you consider your career in hydrology:

- Cooperative education programs. These are offered to high school, college, and graduate students for a period of one year. With a written agreement from both the participating school and the U.S. Geological Survey, the student may alternate between study and employment.
- Student appointments. If you are working on your diploma or degree, you can work with scientific, technical, or professional employees up to 1,040 hours per year. You may work either full or part time.
- Graduate school appointments. If you are in graduate school, you could work full or part time on a professional, analytical, or scientific basis.

- Federal Junior Fellowship program. If you are a high school student in the upper 10 percent of your class and about to enter college, you may qualify for summer employment while in college. You have to be a full-time student in financial need.
- Stay-in-School program. If you are 16 through 21 years old and in financial need, you could qualify for part-time work during the school year (20 hours per week or 40 hours on vacations).
- Minority Participation in Earth Sciences program (MPES). Special funds have been set aside for you if you are a member of a minority group.
- Postdoctoral research grants. If you have received your Ph. D. in earth sciences within the last five years, you may qualify for grants and appointments.
- Faculty member appointments. Full-time and part-time paid appointments for college and university faculty are available for no more than 130 days a year.
- Intergovernmental Personnel Act program. If you are employed by a college or university, you may qualify for assignments to a federal agency for up to two years.

With these programs in place, and state and local governments as possibilities for volunteer and part-time work, you should find ample opportunity to explore the possibilities before you commit to the actual education and training that will be required for full-time employment as a hydrologist. State governments are playing an increasingly more important role in establishing and enforcing regulations to conserve and protect our vital natural resources, including water.

Working alongside hydrologists are hydrologic technicians, who collect, evaluate, compute, and apply their data to various fields. These include engineering, forestry, soil conservation, surveying, and drafting. You may also work in a trade or craft related to hydrological work, such as maintaining equipment.

Geophysicists

What Geophysicists Do

Also working on environmental problems are geophysicists, who study the earth and apply the principles of physics to its atmosphere, oceans, and space environment. Geophysicists also need knowledge of mathematical and clerical principles. They help us find new sources of energy, understand the climate, study the ocean, and investigate the solar system. Geophysicists look for mineral deposits, study the earth's movements, and probe the evolution of oceans.

One example of a study performed by geophysicists is the Global Atmospheric Research Program. This is an international project that has, for the past 20 years, brought many nations together to study atmospheric problems, such as weather patterns and climatic patterns that affect the whole earth.

Planetologists study the solar system to help us understand the earth; seismologists study earthquakes and explosive shocks under the earth in order to understand their causes; volcanologists study the nature of volcanoes and how they affect the earth's structure. These geophysicists all must have a solid grounding in math and natural science. Physics, chemistry, and geology as well as differential calculus are necessary for any undergraduate course of study.

Qualifications and Education

You should have at least 30 semester hours in mathematics and the physical sciences. Twenty of those hours will include geophysics and physics or math.

Geophysicists should have a good general education because they must be flexible, resourceful, and often willing to travel abroad and work with other professionals. Good communication skills, the ability to work on a team, and facility with the computer are almost essential today for employment. Your work may be in a laboratory or in the field.

Job and Salary Outlook

Because of the many energy and environmental problems that exist today, the job prospects for geophysicists are quite good. All aspects of the earth—its structure, evolution, climate, stress capability, and interrelationships—are important to government and private industry. If you have a master's degree, you will be needed in oil and gas companies. Or you may work for consulting engineering firms, waste disposal firms, or industries involved in atmospheric or biospheric enterprises. Your starting salary may be in the $32,000–$35,000-per-year range with a master's degree and $38,000–$42,000 per year with a Ph.D. Federal government agencies that employ geophysicists are the U.S. Geological Survey, the Bureau of Reclamation, the Bureau of Mines, the Bureau of Land Management, and the Minerals Management Service.

Working for the U.S. Bureau of Mines

The U.S. Bureau of Mines of the Department of the Interior deals primarily with research and analysis of virtually everything that has to do with mining of minerals and their use in consumer products. The research focuses on making sure that the country's need for minerals is met and ensuring the safe conditions of mines and processing plants. With all the emphasis on the need to preserve the environment, the bureau also looks for ways to manage the waste produced by turning minerals into products.

The bureau estimates that every American requires 40,000 pounds of new minerals every year. These include lead, zinc, copper, aluminum, iron and steel, and coal. Minerals are needed for cars and cans, on farms, for the military, and for tools and machinery. Developing the technology necessary for these minerals is the job of the bureau.

When research is completed, the data is analyzed and disseminated to various other governmental agencies, industries, and appropriate organizations. Educators, engineers, businesspeople, and executives—all need the information provided by the bureau. This research is not confined to minerals in the United States but rather the world.

Because of the extensive need for minerals, mineral production, and mineral use, the Bureau of Mines employs geologists, metallurgists, engineers, and chemists. The bureau is headquartered in Washington, D.C., but there are research centers and field offices throughout the United States. It disseminates information to the public through publications such as *Minerals Today*, seminars, and films.

Working for Private Industry

If you decide to work for private industry, you may be interested in minerals exploration. In this field, you will try to discover mineral deposits with economic possibilities. If you are a mining geologist, you will turn the mineral that you discover into a profit for your company. You will have to collect and analyze data in order to achieve this. Since you may not get on-the-job training, your education and training are extremely important.

First, you will have to be able to estimate a mineral's economic potential. You will have to submit a written report on your findings, and you should be able to record actual observations that you made in the field. You will have to have course work in mineral deposits to do this, along with metallurgy, exploration geophysics, and mining engineering. Most businesses are requiring a master's degree now and may require a Ph.D. in the near future.

For work in private industry, you may have to start out as a temporary employee or contract geologist. As a permanent employee, you can earn from $30,000–$36,000 per year, and as a temporary, expect about $150–$400 a day. The industry seems to be stabilizing a bit now, but you can expect some ups and downs if you become an explorer of minerals.

Working for State and Local Governments

In the United States, state and local governments are increasingly becoming employers of geoscientists. A recent survey stated that their starting salaries are $17,000–$25,000 a year with a bachelor's degree; $24,000–$30,000 with a master's degree; and $28,000–$38,000 with a Ph.D.

Part of the reason that state governments are employing more people than in the past is because of the many new environmental laws that will require the expertise of environmental scientists who thoroughly know their own fields to assist in enforcement and regulation. States also need people with geologic mapping skills; an ability to assess resources; and the ability to identify natural disasters, such as tornadoes, volcanoes, and earthquakes.

The Association of American State Geologists is working in conjunction with the U.S. Geological Survey to develop a program to map the whole country. This project may also create new jobs at the state level. Since the project will take about 25 years to complete, job security is ensured for those involved.

The U.S. Geological Survey will provide the mapping services that will support national needs while the states will provide state geological surveys. Other support investigations, such as those related to paleontology or petrology, will be conducted. The U.S. Geological Survey will also provide money for colleges and universities for training in this project. When the project is finally authorized, it should begin in 1992.

Working in Consulting

The consulting industry will be a source of employment for quite some time for geologists and hydrologists whose work focuses on the environment. Consulting firms require a master's degree or a bachelor's degree with appropriate field experience.

Consultants are hired to solve specific problems for their clients, which means that their communication skills have to be highly developed. Getting your ideas across in "plain English" may be difficult, but necessary, if the nonprofessional client is to understand them. With that in mind, remember that you may be out in the field one day and back in the office the next.

Other Employers

Geoscientists in general will also find employment in oil, gas, engineering, and construction companies. Our country needs skilled professional people working to preserve the environment, and these same professionals are needed throughout the world, especially in developing countries that need the technological expertise that these scientists can provide. So it is appropriate that those people who work so closely with the resources of the earth should be able to work anywhere on the earth in order to solve resource problems.

Working in Canada

In 1990, a modification of the Canada/U.S.A. Free Trade Act made access to employment for geoscientists in either country possible. You will have to be registered in Canada if you decide to work there. You should contact the Geological Association of Canada before moving. It will provide you with the necessary requirements, regulations, and rules.

Job categories and educational requirements there are similar to those in the United States. Canada is rich in minerals and very concerned about the environment. Canadians are very aware of the need for conservation because of increasing world population, a decreasing supply of natural resources, natural disasters, and man-made catastrophes.

Because of these factors, jobs for earth scientists, both here and in Canada, should be plentiful. If you are well educated in your field; if you have a broad base of academic courses, such as history, languages, and economics; if you are willing to volunteer for fieldwork while you attend school; and if you are versatile enough to be able to combine fields in order to work effectively for the environment, either country should be happy to employ you.

In Canada, it is estimated that 80 percent of earth scientists are employed in the petroleum and mining industries. Here they get necessary training, usually working at first outside of cities. You may work in the mountains or in mines or at oil drilling sites. You would then move up to supervisory positions. Those with a strong background in math, physics, and chemistry are usually employed by consulting firms. Others may be employed to solve environmental problems, either for consultants or the government. Supervisory, research, and development projects follow with experience. Oil, gas, and coal industries are base industries for geoscientists in Canada.

Thinking about a Career in the Earth Sciences

If you're still interested in a career in the earth sciences, you are going to have to commit yourself to your education. You may also want to ask yourself a few questions:

- Do you have an analytical mind?
- Were science courses among your favorites in school?
- Do you like to travel?
- Can you present your ideas coherently?
- Do you mind working outdoors in all kinds of weather?
- Do you work well as part of a team?
- Do you like to share you ideas?
- Are you a problem solver?

- Are you curious about the earth and all its changes?
- Are you flexible?

If you can answer "yes" to these questions, you are ready to look into the geosciences and the career possibilities in both government and industry, in the United States, Canada, or throughout the world. The earth is truly your natural environment, and your job possibilities are excellent.

For Further Information

The Geological Society of America, 3300 Penrose Place, P.O. Box 9140, Boulder, CO 80301
> Publication: *Future Opportunities in the Geological Sciences*

Society for Exploration Geophysicists, P.O. Box 702740, Tulsa, OK 74170
> Publication: *Careers in Exploration Geophysics*

American Geological Institute, 4220 King Street, Alexandria, VA 22302
> Publications: *Directory of Geoscience Departments*
> *Careers in Geology*

Chronicle Guidance Publications, Aurora Street, P.O. Box 1190, Moravia, NY 13118-1190
> Publications: Chronicle Occupational Briefs and Occupational Reprints: "Geophysicists"
> "Groundwater Professionals"
> "Hydrologists"
> "Meteorologists"
> "Oceanographers"
> "Petrologists"

American Geophysical Union, 2000 Florida Avenue, NW, Washington, DC 20009
> Publications: *Careers in Geophysics*
> *Careers in Oceanography*
> *Our Home Planet*

American Association of Petroleum Geologists, P.O. Box 979, Tulsa, OK 74101

U.S. Department of the Interior, 1849 C Street, NW, Washington, DC 20240

Office of Historically Black College and University Programs and Job Corps, 18th and C Streets, NW, Room 2759, Washington, DC 20240
> Publication: *Career Options Handbook*

U.S. Geological Survey, Reston, VA 22092
    Publication: *U.S. Geological Survey: Earth Science in the Public Service*
Water Resources Division, 406 National Center, Reston, VA 22092
U.S. Bureau of Mines, 2401 E Street, NW, Washington, DC 20241
    Publication: Minerals Today
Bureau of Land Management, Division of Cadastral Survey, 18th and C
    Streets, NW, Washington, DC 20240
National Oceanic and Atmospheric Administration, Washington Science
    Center, Building 5, 6010 Executive Boulevard, Rockville, MD 20852
Minerals Management Service, Office of Public Affairs, U.S. Department of
    the Interior, Washington, DC 20240
U.S. Department of Energy, 1000 Independence Avenue, SW,
    Washington, DC 20585
Army Corps of Engineers, 200 Massachusetts Avenue, NW, Washington,
    DC 20314
Geological Association of Canada, Department of Earth Sciences, Memorial
    University of Newfoundland, St. John's, Newfoundland A1B 3X5,
    Canada
The Canadian Geoscience Council, Department of Earth Sciences, Univer-
    sity of Waterloo, Waterloo, Ontario N2L 3G1 Canada
    Publication: *Explore Careers in Geoscience*
Alternative Sources of Energy, 107 South Central Avenue, Milaca, MN
    56353
American Gas Association, 1515 Wilson Boulevard, Arlington, VA 22209
American Institute of Physics, 335 East 45th Street, New York, NY
    10017-3483
American Petroleum Institute, 1220 L Street, NW, Washington, DC 20005
Americans for Energy Independence, 1629 K Street, NW, Suite 500,
    Washington, DC 20006
Amoco, 200 East Randolph Drive, Chicago, IL 60601
Center for Alternative Mining Development Policy, 210 Avon Street, #9,
    La Crosse, WI 54603
Center for Energy Policy and Research, c/o New York Institute of Technol-
    ogy, Old Westbury, NY 11568
Chevron Corporation, 225 Bush Street, San Francisco, CA 94104
Congressional Coal Group, 343 Cannon House Office Building,
    Washington, DC 20515
Conservation and Renewable Energy Inquiry and Referral Service, P.O.
    Box 8900, Silver Spring, MD 20907
Consumer Energy Council of America Research Foundation, 2000 L Street,
    NW, Suite 802, Washington, DC 20036
Council of Energy Resource Tribes, 1580 Logan Street, Suite 400, Denver,
    CO 80203
Energy Research Institute, 6850 Rattlesnake Hammock Road, Naples, FL
    33962

Environmental and Energy Study Institute, 122 C Street, NW, Washington, DC 20001

Exxon Corporation, 1251 Avenue of the Americas, New York, NY 10020

Get Oil Out, P.O. Box 1513, Santa Barbara, CA 93102

Gulf Corporation, P.O. Box 1166, Pittsburgh, PA 15230

Health and Energy Institute, P.O. Box 5357, Takoma Park, MD 20912

Institute of Gas Technology, 3424 South State Street, Chicago, IL 60616

Interstate Oil Compact Commission, P.O. Box 53127, Oklahoma City, OK 73152

Jobs in Energy, 1120 Riverside Avenue, Baltimore, MD 21230

Mobil Corporation, 150 East 42d Street, New York, NY 10017

National Coal Association, 1130 17th Street, NW, Washington, DC 20036

National Petroleum Council, 1625 K Street, NW, 6th Floor, Washington, DC 20006

Occidental Petroleum, 10889 Wilshire Boulevard, Los Angeles, CA 90024

Phillips Petroleum Company, Phillips Building, Bartlesville, OK 74003

Renew America, 1001 Connecticut Avenue, NW, Suite 719, Washington, DC 20036

Shell Oil Company, One Shell Plaza, Houston, TX 77001

Standard Oil Company, 200 Public Square, Cleveland, OH 44114

Texaco, 2000 Westchester Avenue, White Plains, NY 10650

U.S. Energy Association, 1620 I Street, Suite 615, Washington, DC 20006

Pollution Control and Waste Management

T wo of the most crucial tasks for those of you who want to make a career of preserving Mother Earth are pollution control and waste management. Pollution control is nec-essary as a preventive measure in the water, on the land, and in the air. Federal legislation mandates certain regulations, and adhering to them opens up career opportunities.

The Problem of Water Pollution

Water pollution is one of the most serious problems that we face because water recycles itself. We have virtually the same amount of water today that we will have in the future. Therefore, we have to be sure that the water we drink or in which organisms must survive remains pure and clean. This is a difficult task because so much of our water is already polluted, and the danger of acciden-tal pollution in the form of oil spills is always present.

Several laws do help us control damage to our waterways: the River and Harbor Act of 1899, the Water Quality Act of 1965, the Clean Water Restoration Act of 1966, the Federal Water Pollution Control Act Amendments of 1972, the Clean Water Act of 1977, the Safe Drinking Water Act of 1974 (amended in

1977 and 1986), and the Water Quality Act of 1987. All of this legislation provides standards of parity for interstate, coastal, and drinking water. These laws were passed to assure that no industry could discharge pollutant material into water without permission and that waste material would be pretreated so as not to harm city treatment facilities. They also assure the quality of the taste and odor of drinking water and mandate that drinking water be clean enough to prevent disease.

Wastewater has to be treated for reuse in a treatment plant, usually through sewers or septic tanks. Solids are removed, and then the water is purified through certain biological processes. If the water is still not clean enough, further purification is necessary. In the process, sludge is produced, which is often used as fertilizer. Other uses of sludge are being studied.

Careers in Water Pollution Control

Because of the expanding global population and resulting industrial waste, jobs in water pollution control should be quite plentiful in the coming years. Again, a wide range of career opportunities await you, depending on the time you are willing to devote to education and training and whether you want to work for government, industry, or independent organizations. Land planners, citizens, chemists, engineers, technicians, government agencies, private industries, and biologists—all are needed to help reduce waste, to clean up existing waste, and to look for solutions for the future.

Let's start with the possibilities with the federal government and, more particularly, with the Environmental Protection Agency (EPA) to see which jobs are listed for your consideration. We will divide career paths into two categories: water treatment and wastewater treatment careers. Water treatment jobs deal with unused or raw water; wastewater is used water that can be returned to rivers or lakes.

Water Treatment Jobs

Pump-Station Operators

Treatment plants need pump-station operators, whose work will often take them outdoors. Water from rivers, lakes, or other sources has to be pumped to the plant and then to the users of the purified water. Often millions of gallons of water are pumped daily through a series of storage tanks, conduits, and mains. The pumps are operated and controlled by pump-station operators.

All the equipment must be in good working order to allow for the proper amount of pressure, flow, and level of water for the needs of the consumers. Pump-station operators have to know how to conduct tests and keep records of this information. They also have to be able to work with their hands and be familiar with tools.

If you think you would like to be a pump-station operator, you will probably be required to have a high school diploma, preferably with some experience operating and maintaining equipment. You may also want to investigate two-year colleges that offer an associate degree in environmental technology.

You would probably start out as a helper or maintenance worker, during which time you would be trained. After about six months, you might advance to water-treatment plant operator. Most of these jobs are available at city treatment plants.

Water-Treatment Plant Operators

Water-treatment plant operators are similar to pump-station operators, except that they maintain the purity of the water by monitoring panels to check pressure, level, and flow of the water as it moves through the pumps. They must add substances to the water and then test it for purity, clarity, and odor. This operator has to keep accurate records and maintain equipment.

These jobs are usually available at treatment plants in large cities and individual communities. Your job duties may vary according to the size of the facility, and the staff size will also vary. If you work in a very small town, your work may be only part time. Considering, however, all the regulations concerning water quality, these jobs will be plentiful for quite some time.

To become a water-treatment plant operator, you will probably have to have a high school diploma or a comparable mix of education and experience. It is an advantage if you have had some jobs handling machinery and mechanical equipment.

Vocational schools may offer courses in water treatment, and also check community colleges for environmental technology courses. The more education, training, and experience you have, the better your career opportunities will be. You may also be required to take a civil service exam after you have completed your training. Most operators also have to be certified.

As an apprentice, you will have to have 6,000 hours of on-the-job training. In some cases, you may also have to update your knowledge through seminars in order to renew you license. Some states offer courses or specialized training to help you with new technology. These may include aquatic biology, new regulations, or record keeping. You should check with your state licensing board for certification laws and required training.

Your job prospects look good and actually rather steady in the coming years, especially if you continue to update your skills and knowledge. From operator, you could be promoted to foreman, supervisor, or superintendent.

Water Filter Cleaners

Two other technical jobs remain in the water treatment plant: the water filter cleaner and the water meter reader. The water filter cleaner is responsible for keeping the water at the bottom of the filter basin clean. These basins hold layers of gravel and sand through which the water is filtered so that it comes out pure in the end.

The sand and gravel are removed with a suction pipe operated by the filter cleaner, who then hoses the sand and gravel to remove any impurities, scrapes the filter bed, and returns the clean sand and gravel to the bed. You might guess that the filter cleaner has to be physically strong—and you would be right. Filter cleaners often have to work outside the plant in sometimes less-than-comfortable surroundings.

Although this job is extremely important in the water purification process, it doesn't require a great deal of education and training. You would usually only need a grade school education and would then receive a short on-the-job training period. You should, however, be reliable and industrious to tackle this kind of work. Your best employment opportunity will probably be with large filtration plants. This is a good ground-level job to see if you would like to become a mechanic's helper or water-treatment plant operator.

Water Meter Readers

To be a water meter reader, you will most likely have to have a high school diploma, but you can be trained within a few weeks on the job. Your work will be largely outdoors, and in addition to reading meters, you will have to check the meters' working condition, verify records, and turn service on and off. You'll need to be good at arithmetic, keeping accurate records, and detail work.

Wastewater Treatment Jobs

Many of the same processes take place for the treatment of wastewater, but in this case, sewers bring used water to the plant for cleaning and reuse. Many of these plants employ chemists, microbiologists, photo-inspection and TV technicians, and a variety of other workers in addition to plant operators. Since chemists and microbiologists work mainly in laboratories, we'll concentrate on those job opportunities that are found, for the most part, outside the office or laboratory.

Industrial Waste Inspectors

For example, the industrial waste inspector goes to the origin of the pollutants—the industrial or commercial site where the pollutants are treated for disposal—to make sure that permits are valid, that equipment is up to standard, and sometimes to collect samples of the water for testing. Any water source, such as a river, lake, or stream, has to be tested to be sure that harmful pollutants are not discharged into them from a commercial site.

Samples are also collected from sewers and drains and tested in the laboratory. Certain field tests are taken on the spot, such as those for acidity and alkalinity. Most inspectors are also required to take complaints, help industry owners with compliance to regulations, and keep accurate and thorough records in order to calculate any surcharges an offending company may have to pay.

As an inspector, you will be required to do quite a bit of fieldwork and will be exposed to various weather conditions. You will also have to do some light physical work—climbing, walking, crawling, or stretching. Because you are looking for violations of environmental regulations, you must be able to instruct people who are responsible for following the rules while strictly enforcing them. You may be called on to work closely with officers of a company to educate them in federal and state regulations—which can sometimes be confusing—and help them come up with solutions.

To become an industrial waste inspector, you will need to have a good background in wastewater plant operations, know the current environmental regulations, and have a knowledge of equipment and machinery. Very often this is the promotion you will get from wastewater treatment plant operator. And with further education and training, you could become a supervisor or manager. Since water quality control is becoming increasingly important in this country, you should have a steady job, especially in big cities or near large industrial sites.

Industrial Waste Samplers

Industrial waste samplers are workers who go directly to the water source and take used and unused samples to the plant for chemical analysis. These samples are usually taken from suspicious locations, put into tubes or bottles, and labeled with the pertinent information. If the samples indicate that a certain industry has not followed regulations, these samples will help to determine the amount of fines that will be charged to the offending industry.

Sometimes tests are made on site, or monitoring devices are set up to record conditions at specific times and to measure water flow and pressure. Samplers have to be prepared to climb, bend, stretch, and stoop in order to get the samples, so they should be in good physical shape. Both inspectors and samplers need to know how to drive a car and in some cases to operate a small boat.

Some technical training at a vocational high school or courses in wastewater treatment can get you in the door. Then you will have on-the-job training with more experienced personnel. If you want to go further in your career, you will have to get more formal education in wastewater treatment. The outlook for the future is good because of the need to enforce pollution laws and the increasing responsibility of the states in enforcement procedures.

Photo Inspection Technicians

Sewer pipes have to be inspected regularly for maintenance and repairs, and that is the job of the photo inspection technician. This job requires proficiency in the operation of a 35-mm camera, which is used to photograph manholes and record their number, the date, and the weather conditions. This work is done with a crew of sewer workers who set up the equipment over manholes. This equipment allows the camera to move along in the pipe to take pictures.

Light physical work is required as well as the ability to supervise a crew. You will need a high school diploma and a knowledge of sewers and photo equipment. Any additional experience is a plus. From this position, you could advance to supervisor.

Other Technicians in Wastewater Treatment

Other technicians needed for wastewater treatment are the sewage disposal worker, the sewer maintenance worker, mechanic, plant attendant, and TV technician. The wastewater treatment plant operator and the supervisor top the list of further career opportunities in water quality control.

Sewage Disposal Workers

The sewage disposal worker makes sure that all filters, pumps, screens, and tanks are clean by hosing, brushing, and using cleaning solutions. This work is done outdoors for the most part and requires physical stamina, at least an eighth-grade education, and a high degree of reliability and dependability. On-the-job training can be accomplished in about a month.

Sewer Maintenance Workers

Sewers, including manholes, storm drains, and pipes, have to be maintained and repaired on a regular basis, and this is the job of the sewer maintenance worker. They perform routine maintenance as well as replace sections that have worn out. They use power tools, power rodders, high-velocity water jets, and flushers.

This job requires hard, physical labor, such as cutting trees, removing debris, and climbing into manholes. These workers have to bend, stoop, climb, kneel, and crawl in all kinds of weather in the midst of many different, often unpleasant, odors.

A high school diploma is preferred for this work, and you should count on a six-month, on-the-job training period. You could be promoted, after you have accumulated some experience, to lead worker and then to maintenance equipment operator.

Mechanics

The mechanic in the wastewater treatment plant is responsible for the maintenance and repair of all machines and equipment, which include electric motors, turbines, pumps, and blowers. Sometimes they may have to operate the equipment. If you decide to become a mechanic, you'll have to be familiar with power tools, wrenches, and hoists and carry many of them with you as you perform your tasks. This will require some physical strength because you will be crawling, kneeling, and climbing, both inside and outside.

You'll also have to have an aptitude for mechanical work and a high school diploma for this job. Vocational or trade school background is helpful, and there are apprenticeship programs available. With further education, experience, and certification, you could become a superintendent of a wastewater treatment plant.

Television Inspectors

The television inspector has become a valuable technician in the maintenance and repair of sewer systems. Operating a TV camera with chemical sealant, the TV technician inspects and repairs pipes. The technician keeps records and interprets maps and makes repairs. The ability to work with your hands and physical strength are important aspects of this job.

Although job opportunities are generally better for high school graduates, an eighth-grade education could get you a job as an entry-level technician. Then you could get an additional six-month training period on the job. If you want to advance to becoming a TV technician who supervises a work crew, you'll have to have a high school diploma with at least four years' experience in sewer repair work.

Plant Attendants

Plant attendants have to adjust pipe valves, watch temperature and flow rates, turn on steam valves, and inform the superintendent of any trouble. Sometimes they are called on to collect samples and repair equipment. They may also have to perform general maintenance work as well as record keeping. Two years of high school are sufficient for the job, with three to six months' training for an entry-level position. With further education and experience, you may qualify for certification for wastewater treatment plant operator.

Wastewater Treatment Plant Operators

This job is similar to that of the water treatment plant operator. These workers control and operate the pumps, pipes, and valves. The flow of water and solid wastes must be monitored in order for the proper amount of chemicals and wastewater to be processed. Pumps and generators have to be stopped and started, and heat and electricity must be provided to the plant itself. In addition, all equipment has to be inspected for possible repairs. This is the work of the operator.

In large plants, the operators may specialize, for example, as a sludge-control operator or sludge filtration operator. In other plants, operators may be called on to do general maintenance of buildings, perform laboratory tests, and be on call for emergencies.

As a plant operator, you may be working in all kinds of weather, and you may be crawling, climbing, kneeling, and crouching on the job. You will also have to know how to use common and specialized tools and be able to read blueprints.

You'll need a high school diploma and two years' experience in equipment maintenance. If you enter an apprenticeship program, you'll get courses in mathematics, physics, and chemistry. You may also need three years' experience in addition to this classroom training. If you attend a two-year college, you should get an associate's degree in environmental technology. Courses include math, social science, communication skills, report writing, and wastewater treatment. You will have to pass a written test for certification in most states.

Job possibilities as a wastewater treatment plant operator look bright for the future, especially in large cities and as state employees, mainly because of the increasing awareness and new regulations both on the local and state levels.

Supervisors

Supervisors of water and sewer systems are in charge of planning and coordinating all activities in the sewage system, including excavating culverts, installing sewer mains, drilling taps, and making street repairs. As a supervisor, you'll have to keep accurate records, read land plots, order materials, and maintain and repair all equipment. Much of your work will have to do with executing projects and supervising the work of others.

Most of your work will be done outdoors and will demand good physical strength, eyesight, and hearing. A high school diploma is preferred, but you can rise through the ranks to become a supervisor. An aptitude for mechanics, mathematics, or shop in a trade or vocational school is very helpful.

Estuarial Technicians

Other technicians are needed in water quality control, such as the estuarine resource technician and the water pollution control technician. Estuaries, such as bays, inlets, and lagoons, need to be studied for quality because of the rich variety of wildlife that they maintain. As an estuarial technician, you may have to wear diving gear to collect water samples for laboratory analysis. You will also be responsible for writing reports, working with other professionals, and operating instruments that are used in collecting samples.

A two-year associate's degree with course work in math, biology, marine instrumentation, chemistry, and English is helpful. You should also have laboratory work, ecology, and statistical analysis courses. You will probably have to have a bachelor's degree to be promoted.

Water Pollution Control Technicians

Water pollution control technicians take samples from a variety of water sources, monitor flow and other information, operate measuring devices, and conduct on-site chemical and physical tests to help control pollutants in raw or used water. They then have to write up thorough reports of this fieldwork. They often have to interpret computer printouts, prepare statistical analyses of the results, and prepare materials to be used by engineers, scientists, or environmentalists. Most of their work is done outdoors, sometimes under difficult conditions. Therefore, good physical condition is important as well as the ability to travel a great deal.

An associate's degree in chemical technology or science is recommended for this job. It is also important to have at least one year's experience with surveying, measuring, or testing equipment. College courses should include math, natural sciences, chemistry, biology, and engineering. You will receive training with an engineer or scientist and could achieve advancement with a bachelor's degree in engineering or science.

Environmental Engineers

Engineering professionals are in great demand for water-quality control careers. Both government and industry are looking for environmental engineers. They design water and wastewater treatment plants, operate pollution control facilities, and recycle industrial waste to conform to government regulations. They research safe levels of chemicals in water supplies, monitor wastewater treatment processes, and work with fishery and wildlife personnel. They do this to protect fish and wildlife from pollution as well as to look for other sources of water during periods of drought.

Other engineers concerned with environmental problems are sanitary engineers, hydraulic engineers, oil pollution control engineers, and civil engineers, who deal primarily with waterways, irrigation problems, and coastal and waterway pollution.

Sanitary Engineers

Sanitary engineers are responsible for sewage disposal, water pollution control, or water supply problems. They also assist in watershed development and aqueduct and filtration plant construction. Sewage problems involving waste treatment plants are investigated, samples are taken, and evaluations made. These engineers may also be in charge of water supply programs for government agencies. They sometimes work at construction sites, where they advise industrial and civic leaders about wastewater treatment regulations and develop waste treatment programs.

In college, you should graduate as a civil engineer and then take a master's degree in sanitary engineering. Or you may have chemical, structural, or public health engineering as an undergraduate major. Most states require that you be registered and licensed before you start your career. As a sanitary engineer, your services will be needed in private industry as consultants to architectural firms or for major municipal wastewater treatment plants, environmental organizations, and health departments.

Hydrologic Engineers

Hydrologic engineers deal with construction of dams, aqueducts, and reservoirs for the use and control of water supplies. They study soil drainage, flooding, and conservation and analyze droughts, storms, and flood runoff records to forecast and prevent floods and plan for water storage during periods of drought. Some specialize in irrigation projects for agricultural purposes. Hydrologic engineers need a bachelor's degree in civil engineering and should have two years' experience in related work.

Oil Pollution Control Engineers

Oil pollution control engineers are responsible for prevention and control of oil spills when possible. In worst-case scenarios, when the spill actually occurs, they then plan for the cleanup and disposal of the spill.

Prevention of oil spills is probably impossible, but engineers can determine monitoring and maintenance programs for equipment and machinery and develop inspection programs for personnel to check for leaks and malfunctions. Engineers inform appropriate personnel about tides, currents, and wind patterns; they monitor those sites where oil spills might occur; and they can help gas station attendants know how to control and monitor spills in tanks, drains, and catch basins.

Plans for containment and cleanup of oil spills, once they occur, have to be made individually, sometimes depending on whether they are on or offshore. But the engineers' decisions have to be made immediately, according to how fast the oil is dispersed, what the velocity of the wind is, and how fast the water current is. The shape of the spill and length of time that it will take to get all the contractors and helpers to the site have to be considered. Often training drills with a crew will have to take place beforehand to estimate response time in case of emergency.

In the cleanup process, the engineer has many things to think about: keeping accurate records, collecting samples, informing wildlife agencies if necessary, maintaining all environmental rules and regulations, coordinating with local fire departments, and alerting local authorities to the potential hazards to water sources in the affected areas. After the cleanup, the engineer arranges for disposing of the recovered oil. Some of your work would be indoors, but in emergencies, you would be called on to work at the site of the spill, sometimes in bad weather and unpleasant conditions.

A combination of a bachelor's degree in petroleum, chemical, or civil engineering and a long career in all phases of pollution control are necessary for the job of oil pollution control engineer. Then you will be qualified to work for oil companies; contractors who specialize in cleanup; and any federal or state governmental agency that is responsible for the prevention, control, cleanup, and disposal of oil spills.

Civil Engineers

Civil engineers who study the physical control of water work to prevent floods, direct river flow, and control water supply for irrigation purposes. If canals, locks, or hydroelectric power systems are needed, they construct them.

Other careers associated with supplying water for irrigation are basin operators, ditch riders, and watershed tenders. Basin operators remove silt and sand from river water before the water can be used. They may operate certain equipment and keep records. Ditch riders help determine how much water is needed and how long it will be needed. They often have to patrol areas to look for leaks or impediments, clear brush, or repair gauges and meters. Watershed tenders control water flow from reservoirs through the use of gauges and meters. They also keep records, maintain equipment, and solve problems.

All these careers concerned with providing quality water to controlling its flow to cleaning it up after disasters show a concern for the tenuous nature of one of our most valuable natural resources. Large numbers of professionals   and technicians are needed now and in the future to maintain water purity for agricultural, residential, commercial, and industrial use.

The Problem of Land Pollution

The land is also abused in many ways on a daily basis throughout the world. One of the most pressing problems at the moment is garbage disposal. We are presently producing more solid waste than we can dispose of. The words *dumping* and *landfill* are familiar to all of us. Ordinary garbage pollutes the land and groundwater and the contaminants are carried through the air by insects outside the dump itself. Dumps become a health hazard to humans, housing disease-causing rodents and vermin.

More dangerous to the land are the hazardous waste sites, which can be found throughout the country. A monumental job lies ahead for environmental professionals in disposing of such waste, containing it, or converting it to nonhazardous substances. These solid waste problems are so dangerous to the survival of our planet that it will take a concerted effort on the part of every consumer, industry, grass-roots organization, environmental professional, and government agency to turn things around for this good earth.

There are laws on the books now which are helpful, but the problem deserves the total commitment of all citizens to accomplish the kinds of results we need. In 1965, the Solid Waste Disposal Act opened the door for the development of programs that tackled the problem of disposal and provided states with financial and technical aid to carry them out.

The Resource Conservation and Recovery Act of 1970 provided financial aid to construct disposal facilities and research possibilities for the management of solid waste. The Research Conservation and Recovery Act of 1976 further expanded on recovering energy from disposed materials and establishing regulations for the management of hazardous wastes. The Superfund was established specifically to clean up hazardous waste sites that are already in existence. An understanding of these and other federal and local laws is crucial to anyone interested in working for the preservation and purification of Mother Earth.

Individual states are becoming more and more responsible for environmental protection of their area. Part of this mission is to recover resources and energy that had been discarded. Local governments and grass-roots organizations and individual companies are setting up recycling centers in most cities. And garbage collecting in many areas is separated for more rapid recycling. Sanitary landfills have become the norm so that solid waste is disposed of within layers and then covered over to reduce pollutants. Consumers are demanding of manufacturers that they reduce their packaging, and whole industries have at least become aware of the "green revolution." Citizens are now very aware of how dangerous nuclear waste sites are to their health and well being.

Careers in Land Pollution

Waste Management Engineers

Careers with solid waste management and hazardous waste cleanup are many. At the forefront are waste management engineers, who study specifications and plans, inspect disposal facilities, recommend the best ways to process and dispose of garbage, and develop recovery resources programs. They have to write reports and advise appropriate people in government or industry on rules and regulations regarding waste disposal.

A combination of a bachelor's degree and waste management work experience or a master's degree in waste management engineering will qualify you for a position in this field. With growing interest in this area, your prospects for a solid career are very good.

Waste Management Specialists

Alongside the engineers are the waste management specialists. Although they don't design programs, they inspect landfills, confer with appropriate health officials, advise those who operate sanitary landfills on improved methods of disposal, take complaints, and prepare reports. You can qualify for this position with a bachelor's degree in environmental science or civil, sanitary, or chemical engineering. Some experience in solid waste management is preferred.

The Problem of Air Pollution

The air that we and other species depend on for life is also being polluted—with recent EPA estimates as high as 200 million tons of fumes and soot per year in the United States alone. Cars, houses, and smokestacks add carbon monoxide, sulfur dioxide, lead, asbestos, and even arsenic to the air we breathe. Our lungs are at risk on a daily basis when we inhale the smoke from cigarettes or are exposed to radon or asbestos in the buildings we live or work in.

Nuclear accidents like Three Mile Island and Chernobyl further add to the problem. Prevention and control of air pollution is a top priority here and in every country in the world.

The Clean Air Act of 1970, with amendments in 1974 and 1977, was designed to force states to develop programs to control air pollution in order to conform to federal standards for clean air. Even now we do not have the ozone and carbon monoxide problems solved, even though most other pollutants, such as nitrogen dioxide and sulfur dioxide, are now within federal standards.

Ozone depletion is associated with the greenhouse effect, which is seen by many to be a top priority for all air pollution professionals. Toxic wastes, such as dioxin and PCBs, also contribute to hazardous health conditions. All this is combined with the problems of pesticides, radon, and other carcinogenic compounds found in inside air to form a monumental global crisis.

Careers in Air Pollution

Air Quality Engineers

Now if you are feeling committed enough to explore the career possibilities in air quality and pollution control, you should know that the need for environmental professionals is great and will be in the future. For example, air quality engineers are needed in governmental agencies, private industry, oil refineries, electric power plants, and in consulting firms. Their responsibilities include visiting industrial sites, investigating trouble areas, making recommendations for improvements, and setting deadlines for compliance. They also plan new construction, with reduction of pollution as a primary objective. These plans may be for a commercial plant, power plant, or highway. They consider traffic patterns, climate, housing, and even wind direction when making recommendations for new construction.

Some air quality engineers design testing devices, devise new pollution-reducing processes, or explore ways to remove pollutants from certain substances. They work indoors and outdoors, are on call in emergencies, and have the ability to solve problems and do research. Many have to travel to specific sites on a regular basis and often have to climb, lift, and otherwise perform in various climatic conditions.

To qualify as an air quality engineer, you'll have to have a bachelor's degree in engineering and be certified as a professional engineer. If you work for the government, you will have to pass the civil service exam.

Air Quality Specialists

Air quality specialists go into the field to inspect, test, and analyze pollution sources, take samples of soil and other materials affected by air pollution, and write up reports and recommendations. They assist in environmental impact statements, take complaints on hazards caused by toxic waste, and assist in enforcing environmental protection regulations.

A bachelor's degree in science, engineering, environmental health, or statistics is necessary to qualify as an air quality specialist. You should study chemistry, physics, and biology as an undergraduate. Knowledge of computers, public administration, and environmental studies is also beneficial. You will probably also receive on-the-job training whether you work for the government, industry, or consulting firms.

Air Quality Technicians

Air quality technicians assist engineers and scientists by collecting air samples, testing them for pollutants, and recording the information. They inspect pollution sources, test air quality, and operate electronic equipment. Much of this work is done on site and often involves repairing equipment, drawing graphs, and making mathematical equations.

You may prefer to specialize in meteorological work as an air quality technician. As such, you would work with meteorologists in forecasting levels of air pollution. You would work at test sites to check equipment and record temperatures, wind velocity and direction, and pressure. You would assist the meteorologist in setting up weather instruments, performing mathematical calculations, and working with maps and graphs.

You will need two years of college or technical training. This should include laboratory, mechanical, and electrical experience. You will also have to know air quality regulations.

The time is now for you to get involved in pollution control and waste management. No three areas could be more important than the water, the land, and the air for the preservation, conservation, and redemption of our environment. No cause could be more important than cleaning up and purifying those elements that allow us to live.

For Further Information

American Chemical Society, Education Division, 1155 Sixteenth Street, NW, Washington, DC 20036

American Clean Water Project, 107 Spyglass Lane, Fayetteville, NY 13066

American Society of Limnology and Oceanography, Virginia Institute of Marine Science, College of William and Mary, Gloucester Point, VA 23062

American Society of Civil Engineers, 345 East 47th Street, New York, NY 10017

American Water Resources Association, 5410 Grosvenor Lane, Suite 220, Bethesda, MD 20814

American Water Works Association, 6666 West Quincy Avenue, Denver, CO 80235

Association of State and Interstate Water Pollution Control Administrators, 444 North Capitol Street, NW, Suite 330, Washington, DC 20002

Association of State Drinking Water Administrators, 1911 North Fort Myer Drive, Suite 400, Arlington, VA 22209

Great Lakes United, State University College at Buffalo, 1300 Elmwood Avenue, Buffalo, NY 14222

Water Pollution Control Federation, 601 Wythe Street, Alexandria, VA 22314

Acknowledgments

Maureen Delaney, Chief
National Recruitment Program
Office of Human Resources
U.S. Environmental Protection Agency

Maxine C. Millard
Personnel Officer
U.S. Department of the Interior
Geological Survey

Stanley J. Morgan
Acting Chief, Division of Personnel
U.S. Department of the Interior
Bureau of Mines

Beth Nalker
Program Assistant
Office of Environmental Awareness
Smithsonian Institution

National Park Service
Midwest Region
U.S. Department of the Interior

U.S. Fish and Wildlife Service
U.S. Department of the Interior

Darla K. Humrich
Personnel Staffing Specialist
Bureau of Reclamation
U.S. Department of the Interior

Forest Service
U.S. Department of Agriculture

Eileen B. Mason, Office of Personnel
U.S. Nuclear Regulatory Commission

National Zoological Park
Smithsonian Institution

Leann J. Malison
Career Development and Placement Coordinator
American Society of Agronomy

John B. Dewitt
Save-the-Redwoods League

George F. Mitchell
Executive Director
Northeastern Loggers Association, Inc.

Christine Altman
Grants Administrator
Sport Fishing Institute

Fish America Foundation

David Nickum
American Fisheries Society

Arlene Power
Publications Manager
Geological Association of Canada

T. Michael Moreland, Manager
Membership Services
The Geological Society of America

Geological Society of America

American Geophysical Union

American Geological Institute

American Association of Petroleum Geologists

The American Ornithologists' Union

The American Chemical Society

Lori A. Essert
Education Assistant
Water Pollution Control Federation

Roberta S. Proper
Human Resources Representative
Chemical Waste Management, Inc.

National Environmental Health Association

American Society of Civil Engineers

The American Chemical Society
Education Division
Center for Neighborhood Technology

Marianne Millman
Technical Consultant

Lighthawk
The Environmental Air Force

Ben Northcutt
Executive Director
International Erosion Control Association

The American Institute of Biological Sciences

The Wildlife Society, Inc.

John Carney
Public Information
Environmental Defense Fund

Joan A. Schroeder
Executive Secretary
National Association of Environmental Professionals

Shannon A. Horst
Director of Public Awareness
Center for Holistic Resource Management

H.W. Riecken
Director of Administration
Wildlife Habitat Enhancement Council

The National Wildlife Federation

International Association of Fish & Wildlife Agencies

Sierra Club

Tara Faud
Research Assistant
Public Affairs Office
The Ecological Society of America

The American Association of Zoological Parks and Aquariums

The American Association of Zoo Keepers

Don Bixby
American Minor Breeds Conservancy

VGM CAREER BOOKS

VGM Career Horizons
a division of *NTC Publishing Group*
4255 West Touhy Avenue
Lincolnwood, Illinois 60646-1975

Date Due

Nov, 12			
Nov. 20			
11-1			